GOD
ALL THAT MATTERS

Mark Vernon

GOD

Mark Vernon

Hodder Education

338 Euston Road, London NW1 3BH.

Hodder Education is an Hachette UK company

First published in UK 2012 by Hodder Education

British Library Cataloguing in Publication Data: a catalogue record for this title is available from the British Library.

Library of Congress Catalog Card Number: on file.

10 9 8 7 6 5 4 3 2 1

The publisher has used its best endeavours to ensure that any website addresses referred to in this book are correct and active at the time of going to press. However, the publisher and the author have no responsibility for the websites and can make no guarantee that a site will remain live or that the content will remain relevant, decent or appropriate.

The publisher has made every effort to mark as such all words which it believes to be trademarks. The publisher should also like to make it clear that the presence of a word in the book, whether marked or unmarked, in no way affects its legal status as a trademark.

Every reasonable effort has been made by the publisher to trace the copyright holders of material in this book. Any errors or omissions should be notified in writing to the publisher, who will endeavour to rectify the situation for any reprints and future editions.

Hachette UK's policy is to use papers that are natural, renewable and recyclable products and made from wood grown in sustainable forests. The logging and manufacturing processes are expected to conform to the environmental regulations of the country of origin.

www.hoddereducation.co.uk

Typeset by Cenveo Publisher Services.

Printed in Great Britain by CPI Group (UK) Ltd, Croydon, CR0 4YY.

Contents

Acknowledgements

The author and publishers would like to thank the following for their permission to reproduce photos in this book. **Introduction:** http://commons.wikimedia.org/wiki/File:Kircher-Diagram_of_the_names_of_God.png (public domain) (page vii); **Chapter 1:** http://commons.wikimedia.org/wiki/File:Lawrence_Alma-Tadema_10.jpeg (public domain) (page 5); http://commons.wikimedia.org/wiki/File:Dunhuang_Mara_Budda.jpg (public domain) (page 11); **Chapter 2:** http://commons.wikimedia.org/wiki/File:Illustrerad_Verldshistoria_band_I_Ill_175.png (public domain) (page 21); © Det Kongelige Bibliotek. The Royal Library, Denmark (page 24); **Chapter 3:** Library of Congress, Prints & Photographs Division, New York World-Telegram and the Sun Newspaper Photograph Collection, LC-DIG-ppmsca-05649 (page 33); © Olya Yashina – Fotolia (page 35); **Chapter 4:** http://commons.wikimedia.org/wiki/File:William_James_in_1890s.jpg (public domain) (page 47); **Chapter 5:** The Thomas Fisher Rare Book Library, University of Toronto (page 63); © 2010 SuperStock (page 67); **Chapter 6:** © M.Rosenwirth – Fotolia (page 82); **Chapter 7:** © Vaclav Janousek / Fotolia.com (page 96); **Chapter 8:** Welleschik/http://commons.wikimedia.org/wiki/File:Teresa_von_Avila_Bernini1.JPG/http://creativecommons.org/licenses/by-sa/3.0/deed.en (page 106); © SuperStock (page 111).

About the Author

Mark Vernon is a journalist, broadcaster and author of several books. He is the editor-in-chief of the *Chambers Dictionary of Beliefs and Religions* and an honorary research fellow at Birkbeck, University of London, and has degrees in physics and theology and a PhD in philosophy. He used to be a priest in the Church of England, but left a convinced atheist, though then had to admit he is too drawn by spiritual concerns not to take religious traditions and practice seriously – a journey he has written about in his book *How to Be an Agnostic.* For more, including recent articles and events, see www.markvernon.

Introduction

There is a tradition in theology, stretching widely across different religions, of ascribing many names to God. Muhammad advised his followers of God's 99 names. In Judaism there are perhaps 72. The Mahabharata of India is said to contain a thousand names of God. God is All-Wise, Good, Life, Being, Darkness, Almighty, Merciful, Endless, Judge of All, Compassionate, Spirit, Mother, He, Lord, I Am, Master of the Day of Doom, and so on and so on.

The names of God are depicted in labyrinthine diagrams, wheel-like objects around which the plurality of the divine descriptions whirl with dizzying rapidity. They distil gradually as they reach the centre, where typically there is a void or silence.

Denys the Areopagite, in the Christian tradition, stresses that the reason there are many names for God is that God is, in truth, above any naming. The superfluity of names is designed to ensure that we never settle on any one. In *The Mystical Theology*, he writes:

> *Unknowing, or agnosia, is not ignorance or absence of knowledge as ordinarily understood, but rather the realization that no finite knowledge can fully know the Infinite One, and that therefore He is only truly to be approached by agnosia, or by that which is beyond and above knowledge.*

There is a nice irony that 'agnosia', today, describes a medical condition whereby individuals lose the ability to recognize people or things. It is a stressful condition,

▲ The Oedipus Aegyptiacus is a Renaissance synthesis of many of the names of God, displayed here in diagrammatic form.

though in theology, when it comes to God, it might be regarded as a necessary condition. The unknowability implied by the many divine names is an issue we return to when we consider what it means to call God good and to say that God is love.

Another reason God is ascribed many names is that God's attributes and qualities are multiple too. Humankind may know of God in manifold ways, often self-contradictory. Such is the joyous exuberance of the divine, an ecstatic, chaotic spilling-out of creativity and life. It is a feature of the divine nature that we shall consider when we ask whether God is the same as nature and whether God will come at the end of time.

My aim has been to address the central, contemporary questions that I imagine concern searchers for the divine, also known as theologians, be they students, spiritual enquirers or the interested and curious. I've taken a global view, embracing ideas about God from all the main world religions. Difficult questions such as suffering, pressing questions such as ecological concerns, and modern questions such as the death of God are asked too. We will also look at novel ideas about God that are emerging, perhaps unexpectedly, in an age of science and evolution.

This is a short book about a subject that, in terms of magnitude, could claim to be rivalled by no other. God is called the Infinite. To those who trust and yearn for God, God is ultimately all that matters.

1

Is God in
suffering?

Where is God when people are suffering? We begin with this perennial question because it is both the major obstacle that modern individuals have to belief in God and one that will surely not go away for so long as there is pain, loss and evil in the world. And you can be sure that events and attitudes that mar life will exist whilst there is life, for with life always comes one eventuality: death.

In some ways, attempting to resolve this question in a rational way is offensive in itself. In the book of Job, in the Hebrew Bible, Job's friends offer explanations for why he has been plagued with boils and sores, the annihilation of his family and the destruction of his goods.

Their themes are that God is righteous, not evil, and saves good people, so Job must have done something wrong. Or they argue that human beings are by nature repulsive to the holiness of God and that punishment is a form of purification. Or that God does not care for sinners. Or that we simply can't understand and as mere mortals should not expect to. Job is tortured by their platitudinous remarks; hence the colloquialism 'the patience of Job'. Their efforts are dehumanizing of Job's dreadful, agonizing reality. Anger at them and God surges up inside him. Little wonder that the novelist Louis de Bernières has called Job's comforters 'possibly the most irritating characters in all of literature'. This is a powerful warning to anyone who is tempted to understand what is often referred to as the 'problem of evil' – how a good, all-powerful God can allow malevolence in the world He created.

That said, when a firm eye is kept on the limitations of the task, some possibly useful reflections might emerge. It is not that they solve the problem. In a way, they deepen it, though in a particular way: by deepening an understanding of what it means to be human. That may offer dignity, if not release, by finding meaning in the darkness.

There are two traditional responses to the problem of evil. The first of these is known as the free-will defence, stating that suffering is a consequence of the fact that God has made human beings free to act, and therefore to act in bad ways as well as in good ways. Human freedom is a great good, for it means that we can be ourselves, not divine puppets. The price we pay, though, is pain.

The second is known as the instrumental defence, and tries to make the case that suffering, whilst terrible, is the pathway human beings must tread in their personal development. God is like a mother who must let her child go alone into the world, though she knows the youngster will suffer in it and possibly be broken by it. That is the only way to grow up.

There is something of worth in these defences. It is true that freedom entails mistakes, for possessing freedom is a skill that human beings must learn to deploy well, and there is no better learning experience than when something goes wrong. But it hurts.

Further, as it is part of human nature to be proud and seek self-sufficiency, because these characteristics help us survive, a rightful pride and necessary independence always risk becoming an arrogant and lonely self-satisfaction. That excess may, in turn, be eroded only by the painful realization that we need others. Hence, as the book of Proverbs has it, 'Pride goes before destruction, and haughtiness before a fall'.

All that might be true. And yet, as the philosopher John Cottingham has argued, the heart of the problem of evil for believers in a good God is that there is so much of it. Is genocide a price worth paying for human freedom? Do individuals need to suffer a holocaust to learn humility? The answer is clearly not. The free-will and instrumental defences become offensive when they are presented as conclusive. They then deserve as much odium as Job's ancient comforters.

Cottingham believes there is a more satisfactory, if still modest, alternative. It draws on traditional theodicy too, as the attempt to vindicate God of the existence of evil is known, and in particular the theodicies that have contemplated the ramifications of what it means to be made of matter, the biological stuff of our bodies. In his book, *The Spiritual Dimension*, Cottingham suggests that this discussion is illuminated by the light of what has been discovered in modern science.

The ancient sources of this theodicy might be traced back to Plotinus, the creator of the philosophy known as neo-Platonism. During the last part of his life, Plotinus suffered from malign diphtheria, according to his biographer and disciple Porphyry. 'He became hoarse,' Porphyry writes, 'so that his voice quite lost its clear and sonorous note, his sight grew dim and ulcers formed on his hands and feet.' When his time came to die, his last reported words echoed the substance of his philosophy: 'I have been a long time waiting for you; I am striving to give back the Divine in myself to the Divine in the All.'

Neo-Platonism tends to identify matter with evil. Hence, when Plotinus died, he understood that he was finally shedding his material nature and that the spark of the divine that had animated him in life, his soul which is good, was returning to the divine that permeates all things. This gives us a clue as to the nature of the link between matter and evil. Plotinus believes it is a consequence of the way in which God has ordered the world.

▲ Pandora was the first woman in ancient Greek myth, who opened a box, or jar, from which flew all the evils that would afflict humankind. Only hope was left inside.

In the world, some aspects are close to the Source of all. Plotinus would include the human soul on this list. But not everything can be close if it is to be distinguishable from the divine. In fact, if God created a world that was perfect, logic dictates that it would be identical with God, who alone is perfect. Creation, therefore, contains what the philosopher Leibniz called 'original imperfection', that which makes it less than perfect, a diminution, a corollary of it being created differently from God. The further creation is away from the Source, the more deprived it is of the divine goodness.

Ancient evil

In the pre-Christian world, good and evil tended to be viewed as coming from the gods, and so there was, in a sense, no problem of evil. The existence of evil was simply part and parcel of the inscrutable ways of Zeus and the cohorts of deities. Evils might be sent as a form of punishment for disloyalty to local gods, or an ancestor.

In Greek mythology there is talk of a Golden Age, before suffering, when people had lived without pain and long into old age. The first woman, Pandora, had brought a box into the world from which evils escaped.

Alternatively, the Pythagoreans – no doubt taking up what they had learnt from ancient Indian philosophy – argued that individuals suffer now as a result of the evils they have committed in previous existences. The eternal wheel of samsara, as described in Hinduism, is an endless cycle of birth, suffering, death and rebirth. It can be escaped only by living a good life.

Evil is, therefore, a consequence of the created order. It makes no more sense to complain of bad things like illness than it does to rage against ever being born. In the Enneads, Porphyry's record of Plotinus's life and teaching, Plotinus explains:

> We are like people who know nothing about painting and yet reproach the artist because he did not put pretty colours everywhere, whereas the artist distributed the appropriate colour to each and every spot. Cities, too – even those which have a good constitution – are not made up of equal citizens. It is as if one were to criticize a drama because all the characters in it were not heroes, but it also contained a slave and a foulmouthed hayseed. And yet they make the play complete, and it wouldn't have been any good if you took them away.

Now, you may notice echoes of the free-will and instrumental defences in these remarks, and Plotinus does deploy them, in part. Evil has side-effects, he says, that may be good:

> It wakes us up, and awakens the spirit and intelligence, as we are forced to stand against the inroads of wrongdoing, and it makes us learn how great a good is virtue, by comparison with the evils which are the lot of wrong-doers. Now, it was not for this purpose that evils came about, but since they have come about, the world makes use of them as appropriate.

However, it is the specific way he links matter to evil that is key, and worth separating from those other issues. For, in a certain sense, matter served him well in his life. It enabled him to live. Further, as he used his body in his contemplation of the divine, his biological senses and material imagination were the vehicles through which he arrived at his intimations of God. Indeed, the material world is a rich source of metaphors and analogies for understanding the divine. Plotinus talks of how creation flows out of God like a river: it is in its lower reaches, furthest away from the Source, that it becomes less and less good, like an estuary that is polluted by the time it reaches the sea. Life on earth might be said to be mixed with evil, but life itself is a great good. Hence, he adds, 'It could be said that, in and of itself, life within the body is an evil, but that, thanks to virtue, the soul can come to with the Good.'

The notion that there is a necessary imperfection in creation, which can be identified with its material nature, is called a conception of metaphysical evil. However, Cottingham asks, does that of itself imply the existence of suffering? 'Why should not God have created beings that were only slightly less perfect than himself, but still immortal and wholly free from pain and distress?', he asks – creatures like angels, perhaps.

One response to this thought is known as the principle of plenitude. God's creative love is overflowing. The divine plenitude has the quality of ceaseless activity and that means it cannot not be generative. Further, it is bound to explore all possible forms of creativity, and that will include the material. You might say that because matter can exist, God wills that material creatures should too, for all the flaws, else creation would be less glorious than it might be.

All this, though, begs a question: what is the nature of matter? How is it 'flawed'? Whence its evil? Here, the discussion moves on from ancient insights to the light that science can throw on the question.

Werner Heisenberg, the physicist who was seminal in the development of quantum theory, reflected on this in his book *Physics and Philosophy*. The way that different epochs have understood matter, he remarks, might be taken as defining the different epochs. Early modern science, for example, up to the end of the nineteenth century, understood matter in juxtaposition to forces. Matter is that on which forces can act, and it is productive of forces, like gravity. This is a dualistic conception, as if matter and energy were two different aspects of the world.

But with quantum physics, this dualism collapses. 'Every field of force contains energy and in so far constitutes matter,' Heisenberg explains. 'To every field of force there belongs a specific kind of elementary particle with essentially the same properties as all other atomic units of matter.'

As if that were not shift enough, quantum physics undermines another assumption that it is tempting to make about matter, namely that it is immutable. This was the conclusion that the first atomists drew. Democritus, and his followers, reasoned that if you divide something, and divide it again and again and again, you must eventually reach something that is indivisible. If you did not, you could go on dividing indefinitely, until at infinity you were left with nothing. This cannot be the case as something cannot come out of nothing. Hence, they proposed, the world is composed of indivisible units, in Greek, atoms.

But quantum physics destroys this conception of atoms as powerfully as it undermines physical dualism. Matter is not, at base, immutable. 'All the elementary particles can, at sufficiently high energies, be transmuted into other particles, or they can simply be created from kinetic energy and can be annihilated into energy,' Heisenberg continues. 'All the elementary particles are made of the same substance, which we may call energy or universal matter; they are just different forms in which matter can appear.'

What this means for creatures made of matter is that underlying their existence is a fundamental impermanence. Systems of matter do not stand still: they constantly shift, exchange energy and decay. We are, to a degree, shielded from this fickle volatility because life might be defined as the ability to achieve a degree of material stability amidst the decay, what biologists call homeostasis. However, this equilibrium can only be maintained by balancing and juggling the manifold changes and processes that are the stuff of life. We are dust of the earth, as the book of Genesis has it, and to dust we will eventually return.

Evil in Buddhism

There is no problem of evil in Buddhism as there is no creator God. Further, Buddhists are encouraged not to think of good or evil as intrinsic features of the world. Rather, they are simply the consequences of deeds, which might be positive or negative. This is the law of karma, or cause and effect.

Buddhist mythology does speak of Mara, the tempter or evil one. But Mara encourages the delusion that evil comes from outside the individual. Those who are enlightened, though, know it as created from within. 'By oneself, indeed, is evil done; by oneself is one defiled,' says the Dharmapada.

▲ Mara, the demon above Buddha, is a personification of the death of the spiritual life in Buddhist mythology. He sent his daughters to tempt the Buddha away from the enlightened path.

A number of conclusions about the problem of evil follow from the science, Cottingham explains. First, everything made of matter will be mortal. A subatomic particle may have a tiny half-life; the life cycle of the sun unfolds over billions of years; human existence is measured somewhere in the middle. But mortality is our lot. And if such change and decay, instability and collapse, are features of life as we know it, then 'the human condition is inherently vulnerable, always subject to the possibility of suffering,' Cottingham concludes.

However, he immediately raises an objection. Might not God have created 'better dust'? The answer seems to be negative. God's creativity might be defined as plentiful, but that is not the same as being unconstrained. As is sometimes noted in these kind of discussions, there could not be any such thing as a square triangle. Similarly, according to contemporary science, there cannot be any such thing as immortal matter. 'And that means that human life can no longer be seen as some "special" *sui generis* process,' Cottingham adds, 'which we can then complain that the deity has not organized better, but rather that it has to be recognised as emerging from the cosmic flux of ever-decaying material energy.'

This analysis does nothing to mitigate the agony and tragedy of the worst kinds of suffering. The aim is not to become a modern-day comforter of Job. You might say that it achieves little more than stating the obvious: material life is one of delight and desperation. The modest aim, if the reasoning is not flawed, is to suggest that whilst few would argue that the delights of life are incompatible with belief in God, life's desperate moments can be uncomfortably defended in conjunction with belief in a good creator deity too. This may aid the thinking part of suffering humankind, if not the feeling part.

It is worth saying something about the nature of evil too, that which lies behind so much suffering. Today, it is quite common to resist using the word at all. Some would object that the notion of evil already incorporates theistic assumptions, as if evil is a personal force in the world. Others say that invoking evil as an explanation for what is bad actually just mystifies, so prevents useful explanations.

However, the theological concept of evil, properly understood, is quite specific and might aid even secular discussions. A classic statement is made by the thirteenth-century theological great, Thomas Aquinas, who defines it as a lack of goodness or, in Latin, *privatio boni*. Evil is nothing, almost as described in Edmund Burke's thought, 'It is only necessary for the good man to do nothing for evil to triumph.' It is not the opposite of goodness, but the absence of goodness. The relationship between what is good and what is evil is rather like the relationship between hot and cold: things grow cold when heat is extracted from them; they become absolutely cold when no more heat can be removed. Similarly when what is good is removed.

Extending the definition, evil might be said to exist in situations where there is a lack of value and moral force. Terry Eagleton, in his book *On Evil*, makes the observation that this explains why slime is often used to depict evil in the popular imagination. Slime is physically undifferentiated stuff, and evil is a morally nihilistic state of being.

Similarly, evil might be defined as a lack of virtue, in the sense meant by Aristotle, the virtues being those qualities of habit and character that allow human beings to flourish, to become all they might be. Evil, then, is life as it should not be; as it is supposed not to be.

Another way of defining this lack at the heart of evil comes in modern psychotherapy. Those rare individuals who are said to have done great evil, such as mass murders, often do so as a result of psychotic conditions. The schizophrenic may experience life as a frightening internal invasion of their body. The paranoiac pushes this ill into the world, so may feel attacked from the outside and attack back. Darian Leader, the psychotherapist, makes the point that psychosis may provoke many suffers to do good in the world too: a medic may be motivated to seek cures for microbial invasion; an environmentalist to ridding the planet of the evil of destruction and pollution. However, a small fraction of those with psychosis will commit acts of brutality, an even smaller percentage of spectacular brutality.

What underlies the turn to such extremes is hotly contended, but one partial cause may be a lack of an appropriate attachment to a parental figure. Again, note the lack of something good. The baby learns who it is – even that it is – by the quality of the attachment it forms with its mother or primary carer, according to the studies of the British paediatrician Donald Winnicott. The mother is like a highly reflective mirror: she sees the baby and so the baby learns to see itself. They form an emotional bond that is attuned to the baby's inner life. Only next the baby must learn to become detached from the mother, in order to be a separate maturing self. That provokes a kind of primitive anxiety, though if the baby has a strong enough sense of itself, gained from a good enough quality of attachment, it can survive the trauma and develop a robust sense of who it is. But if the attachment between the parent and child is damaged, perhaps because of separation or because the parent has his or her own history of hurt and so is not able to be attuned to the child's inner life, then the baby may develop permanent psychotic traits. That lack may, in turn, be a cause for what is known as human evil. It is another *privatio boni*.

Aquinas explored this definition of evil because it meant that God is not actively involved in evil. It is in situations where God is absent that evil may flourish. When that is linked to Leibniz's notion of 'original imperfection', another variant on this understanding of the reality of suffering emerges. Evil as a lack of goodness will be part of any world that God creates for the very reason that such a creation must be, to a degree, separate from the divine being.

2

Is God our
moral ideal?

It is said that God is dead. This was Friedrich Nietzsche's famous summary of the western cultural collapse in the believability of grand metaphysical perceptions of God. They had fired minds as diverse as Plato and Avicenna, as Maimonides and Aquinas. Now, Nietzsche declared at the end of the nineteenth century, has come the time when humanity must strive to find its own way in the world. We must move to a state of being beyond the old ideas of a divinely ordained good and evil, to forge a life that is good because we deem it so.

It will be hard. When Nietzsche told the story of a madman who swept into the marketplace and told his peers that God had passed away, he also warned them that a universe without a transcendent horizon, and an earth without the warmth of the divine, is a profoundly cold and disorientating place. Terror is more likely to grip us than joy, should we choose to open our eyes and see the reality of the modern predicament.

A number of philosophical systems across the twentieth century, and now into the twenty-first, have tried to rise to the challenge of life after God. Existentialists argued that a godless universe is a free universe because we are not answerable to anything or anyone but ourselves. Atheistic humanism has adopted the ethic of utilitarianism, which rests its notions of good and evil on pleasure and pain: the aim of life is happiness, defined as the maximization of life's pleasures and the minimization of its agonies. No need for a divine horizon there.

But it would not have surprised Nietzsche that another set of responses to his prophecy have held onto God, only not as a metaphysical reality. Rather, this option imagines God as a dream in humankind's eye. God is the invisible summation of our best ideals, the non-real north pole that can orientate an inner moral compass. Followers of this ilk are likely to maintain many of the traditional practices of religion, its beautiful liturgies and rites of passage, on the grounds that these can inspire the best in us and help us to understand the dizzy experience of being alive. God is dead, though can live on as a helpful fiction, an adult version of Father Christmas for kids.

The non-real God who lives

I suspect that in certain parts of Europe the proposition that God is dead, but that religion is still a magnificent human construction, has substantial appeal. The former Astronomer Royal, Martin Rees, has argued that human beings barely understand the inner life of a hydrogen atom, so it seems excessive to speculate about the reality of God. And yet, he goes to Evensong in the chapel of Trinity College, Cambridge, where he is Master. The novelist Philip Pullman defines himself as a strict materialist and believes that this life is all there is. And yet, he is adamant that the Church of England is 'his tribe'. The philosopher Mary Warnock is an atheist, but writes in her book *Dishonest to God* that there are times in life, such as at moments of death, when religious rituals and traditions hold that excess of feeling better than anything else. She concludes that religious traditions such as of music, whilst not necessary in society, are no less great goods: 'To lose these things, though it might not be the end of society, would be to its incomparable spiritual loss.' Even the vocally atheistic Richard Dawkins has admitted he rather likes Christmas for its cultural resonance and the singing of carols.

Arguably, the individual who has most popularized and developed this option is the theologian Don Cupitt. Following a television series in the 1980s, his Sea of Faith Network garners widespread support from people who feel that they can no longer believe the doctrines of their inherited religious traditions, though sense that they embody something of immense human worth no less.

However, Cupitt and his fellow travellers belong, in a way, to a very ancient tradition. It is one that believes religion is good because it is good for the moral sustenance of humanity. It is worth diving back into history to glimpse the origins of this view of God.

It could be said to start with the Stoics, a school of philosophy that arose in ancient Athens in the century that followed the death of Socrates. For the Stoics, theology was part of physics. God was identified as the underlying principle that governs the cosmos, a notion that was captured in the rich ancient Greek word 'logos'. It is often translated as 'word', as it is in the famous opening sentence of St John's gospel, 'In the beginning was the Word'; or 'discourse', 'reason', 'activity' or 'principle'.

Stoic logos theology addressed itself to issues such as the rational nature of the divine, the proper goals and ends to which the world is directed, and the providential nature of human life. Such deep tendencies were far from immediately obvious in everyday life and, the Stoics argued, may well be concealed by the multiple, popular forms of religiosity that existed around them – the diverse mythologies, superstitious divination, and obscure rites of the Hellenic world.

▲ Zeno of Citium, a trader turned philosopher, is the founder of Stoicism.

Chrysippus, arguably the most important Stoic philosopher, proposed that to understand the logos correctly required a kind of initiation. He wrote:

> *The theories about the gods have to be the last thing to be taught, on top of everything else, when the soul is fortified and strong and able to remain silent in front of the uninitiated. For it is quite a struggle to hear the right things about the gods and to get a hold of them.*

Cicero expressed it this way, in his book *On Ends*: 'Nor again can anyone judge truly of things good and evil, save by a knowledge of the whole plan of nature and even of the life of the gods.' You need a god's-eye view.

The Stoics were natural philosophers in the sense that they believed studying nature, particularly physics, was the way to understand not only the intricacies of the natural world but the complexity of moral life. We are made of the same stuff as the universe, the logic went, and so understanding the principles that govern the world illuminates the principles that govern ethics. In particular, underneath the multiplicity lies the unity and power of the logos that orders the world according to a benign fate.

This meant that Stoic theology was intimately tied to not only physics but also the good life. A crucial reason why we do science, they thought, was because it can teach us how to live. If there is one fundamental that arises from the study of the cosmos it is that everything is determined by God, the logos. As the stars move in fixed patterns across the sky, so is life controlled by fate.

It is providential. It orders all things well. Hence, the main effort in Stoic ethics was to train yourself to 'go with the flow'. When life appears to be going wrong, and a person is suffering, the chances are that the individual is resisting the logos. Like a cylinder that rolls down a hill, Chrysippus proposed, life will include its knocks and bumps. That is only to suffer some inevitable 'collateral damage'.

What we have, though, is a choice as to whether or not to complain. The advice is to learn not to, for complaints only compound the suffering, and you can trust the logos that all in the end will be well because the logos is good. It favourably shapes the moral order. Everything works out well in the end, even when we cannot see it for ourselves. Our task in life is to throw ourselves into life. The Stoic's prayer is that the individual's will and virtue conforms to the underlying will and beneficence of nature. Cleanthes offered this intercession: 'Lead me, O Zeus, and you, Destiny, to wherever you have assigned me to go. I will not falter, and follow; and should I be unwilling, and be bad, I shall follow even so.'

Embrace life, Stoics promised their followers, and you will discover an inner sense of tranquility. This arises because the Stoic can be confident that he is living well because he is living naturally, as the cosmos has shaped him. Science delivers knowledge but it also helps people to be reconciled to the way things are.

Stoics also encouraged the contemplation of the moral order and the vastness of the universe. In this way, an individual might learn to see their life in perspective, and see that the worst problems were probably not so bad. One exercise was to imagine oneself high up in the heavens, gazing back down on earth. In the *Dream of Scipio*, Cicero has Scipio Aemilianus being visited by his famous ancestor, Scipio Africanus. Scipio is afforded a high view of life, and Africanus comments:

> *I perceive that you are now fixing your eyes on the abode and home of men, and if it seems to you small, as it really is, then look always at these heavenly things, and despise those earthly. For what reputation from the speech of men, or what fame worth seeking, can you obtain?*

The vision brings existential relief.

▲ Macrobius's twelfth-century diagrammatic representation of what was revealed in the dream of Scipio.

Religion, then, could be a good thing not so much because it was true but because it helped people to live well. The many gods found in homes and temples might be a happy fiction that rulers and individuals could utilize to ensure their good behaviour. The so-called Sisyphus fragment, a preserved line spoken by a character of that name in a play, expresses the thought well, here translated by R G Bury:

> Some shrewd man first, a man in judgment wise,
> Found for mortals the fear of gods,
> Thereby to frighten the wicked should they
> Even act or speak or scheme in secret.
> Hence it was that he introduced the divine
> Telling how the divinity enjoys endless life,
> Hears and sees, and takes thought
> And attends to things, and his nature is divine,
> So that everything which mortals say is heard
> And everything done is visible.

In other words, God is an all-seeing eye or impartial observer, as the economist Adam Smith was later to call it. That said, the Stoics were not atheists. Instead, the gods of traditional religion, which emerge from the turbulence of the human imagination, could be thought of as reflections, more or less accurate, of the divine logos. As the logos pervades all things, it would also be detected in even the wildest cult or speculation, by the initiated. The names people give to gods, no matter how deluded, are expressions of the ways they encounter providence. Religion is, therefore, to be respected, on the whole.

So how might the true divine be described? A well-known Stoic description of God ran as follows. God is ‘an immortal living being, rational, perfect and thinking in happiness, unreceptive of anything bad and provident with regard to the cosmos and the things therein. But he is not of human form.’ God is rather ‘pure soul’, as natural a constituent of things as the matter of the earth, according to Stoic physics; and the cosmos is ensouled in God.

Stoic theology has had a long run since its Hellenic origins. A number of features appealed to the first Christians when they were searching for ways to unpack the significance of the life, death and resurrection of Jesus. He came to be pictured as the incarnation of the divine logos. Hence, John's gospel begins, 'In the beginning was the Word [the logos]'. They warmed to the notion of a divine reason that makes and sustains all things; the struggle to conform one's will to God's will; a trust in God that could be found in the midst of suffering. St Paul quoted from and borrowed Stoic ideas when he preached to the Athenians in front of the Areopagus, as recorded in the Acts of the Apostles. '[God's] offspring too are we' was a Stoic sentiment he deployed, and he appealed to their sense of determinism and fate when he continued, 'having determined their appointed seasons, and established their habitation'.

The moral rationalism of Stoic theology entered the Jewish tradition too, notably via the writings of Philo of Alexandria, a near contemporary of Jesus. He noted that the word 'logos' appears many times in the Greek version of the Hebrew Bible, and whilst it usually refers to God's personal action or activity, it was ripe for the philosophical development that Philo undertook. He presents God's logos as rational and wise, at least partly within the grasp of the human intellect. The Stoic sentiment of benign determinism is also present in this thought: 'it was owing to the Logos that God was both a ruler and good.'

So the way in which the first Stoics knitted together their conception of physics and theology, ethics and providence, fate and moral order has had a long history. It has evolved and diversified over the centuries. And then we reach the modern world. What happened next might be captured like this. God as a metaphysical entity could no longer be thought to exist. But God as the summation and guarantor of our best ideals, God as the personification of the moral order, remains an invaluable fiction.

Kant and God's regulative function

A crucial moment in the emergence of non-realism came before Nietzsche, in the philosophy of Immanuel Kant, the greatest thinker of the Enlightenment. At the risk of compressing the complexities of his thought, it might be summarized in this way.

He was a theist, but argued that human knowledge is strictly limited to human experience. Theological speculation, then, is flawed, no more so than in its attempts to understand the inner life of God. However, Kant also believed that theological speculation is inevitable. It is hard-wired into the human psyche and arises for the simple but profound reason that we find ourselves to exist. So why is there something not nothing? There is no answer, because the conditions of human existence are simply given, unconditionally. For many, that conclusion leads naturally to thoughts of God.

However, such transcendent ideas and principles of reason are useful because they do contribute to our knowledge of moral life. How so? It is an apparent paradox that resolves this way.

Kant was absolutely certain that human morality must be rational. Only if it were based on reason could people be persuaded to accept it. But part of the reasonableness of morality must be that the moral life is possible. 'Ought implies can', as he punned, though this poses a major problem because human beings clearly find it impossible, or at least very difficult, to live a good life. Moral failure abounds. Why bother, the rational person might therefore ask?

The only way to guarantee that what one should do is actually possible to do is if morality is grounded in the notion of a good God, a moral logos. At least, as it were, there is unalloyed goodness in heaven. Consistent with his conviction that human knowledge is strictly limited to human experience, Kant said that it is impossible to know anything about this good God as God is in Godself. Our knowledge of God is not 'constitutive'. However, our knowledge of God can be 'regulative', meaning that it holds insight enough to guide us in our attempts to live well. To the extent that we can be moral, then, the good person will both believe in and 'know' God.

Don Cupitt borrows from Kant's regulative conception of God, drops the existence of God, and keeps the ideal. He summarizes his position in *After God*, one of his many lucid books:

> *What survives of the old religions, then, is a small number of tricks and techniques of religious existence: ways of being a self and of relating oneself to the whole of which one is part. These*

tricks can help us to love life and live well: that, now, is religion.

He has explored three such 'tricks' in particular. One is the 'Eye of God', or gaining a God's-eye view on your life. It is reminiscent of Scipio's dream. A second is the 'Blissful Void', the sense of tranquillity that arises when you can accept what modern science tells you of existence. Life is nihilistic, yes, in the sense that there is nothing outside of the natural world which lends the natural world meaning. 'Fleeting insubstantial emptiness' is all, Cupitt believes, but with that can come a new levity and lightness: 'The strange unexpected happiness this brings is a wonderful deliverance from the fear of death, loss, and suffering.' Again, it is an atheistic form of Stoicism. Third, he recommends 'Solar Living', that is throwing yourself into life. It is like the old spiritual idea of giving your life to God, though in the non-realist frame, it is particularly like the old Stoic idea of going with the flow.

Unsurprisingly, Cupitt's non-realism has been critiqued by theologians who remain realist about the existence of God. They accuse Cupitt of being unable to live with the necessary uncertainty that theism requires – uncertainty because, by definition, God will lie beyond human grasp: though Cupitt may accuse traditional belief of offering a now unwarranted consolation to the faithful, the decisiveness of his atheism might be said to offer an equally unwarranted consolation too, when it sets worried, sceptical minds at rest, and still allows them a little happy, aesthetically pleasing church-going.

Alternatively, they argue that theological non-realism implies scientific non-realism too, for all that Cupitt rests his case on the supposedly definite findings of the natural sciences. This is because both science and theology presume the cosmos to be rational and reliable, else there could not be laws of nature and the like. But that rationality and reliability must rest on something else, that being what the Stoics called the logos and what the theists call God. An atheistic science that ditches this theological element is, in truth, left without foundations, which is to say that science is more of a theological exercise than many might assume.

There is a third reason that the non-realist view of God might be found wanting. It was highlighted by Rowan Williams, a sometime colleague of Cupitt, when he referred to Simone Weil's definition of God as 'the name we give to the connections we cannot make'. This thought undermines the non-realist confidence that God is a symbol of our own making. It challenges the hubris that presumes God depends on us, not we on God. Williams also wrote that 'the challenge, the dynamism and the critical edge of the notion of an "objective" God are what saves the interior life from indulgence, stasis and insensitivity to the possibilities of self-deceit'. That is to say that fabricators of their own personal divinity are more likely to become deluded than searchers after the real God as they assume nothing outside of themselves to judge themselves against. Or, to put it more succinctly, the risk of affirming that God is dead but still worth imaginatively following is that you reinstate another god in this place: yourself.

3

Is God the same as nature?

Strange as it may seem, there is one realist understanding of God that some atheists find almost believable. In his theism-busting bestseller, *The God Delusion*, Richard Dawkins declares that he is, in fact, religious in one sense. Albert Einstein had once explained: 'To sense that behind anything that can be experienced there is a something that our mind cannot grasp and whose beauty and sublimity reaches us only indirectly and as a feeble reflection, this is religiousness. In this sense I am religious.' Dawkins agrees.

What is this 'something divinity' to which Einstein also referred when he made a number of his best-known remarks, 'God is subtle but he is not malicious' and 'God does not play dice'?

It is the deity of the pantheist, the individual who holds that God and nature are ultimately identical. God is cited as a way of signalling that nature is a truly wonderful phenomenon in that it is shaped by lawful patterns and coordinating balances. Science would not be possible without these deeply embedded traits. Further, you can say that in as much as science depends upon the existence of natural laws, which it aims to uncover, it depends upon a feature of nature that it may never fully understand. Einstein again:

> My religiosity consists of a humble admiration of the infinitely superior spirit who reveals himself in the slight details we are able to perceive with our frail and feeble minds. That deeply emotional conviction of the presence of a superior reasoning power, which is revealed in the incomprehensible universe, forms my idea of God.

Dawkins does draw the line when Einstein confesses that there are things beyond science's comprehension. The arch-atheist neutralizes his pantheism by referring to it as 'sexed-up atheism'. But is Dawkins justified in doing so? If the divine of pantheism is just nature writ large, then why bother using the word 'God' at all? Why not just nature, perhaps with a capital 'N'?

▲ Albert Einstein, the iconic scientist.

Pantheism and animism

It is important to draw a distinction between pantheism and animism. If pantheism is closely associated with monotheism, being the idea that the one God is the totality of nature, animism is the belief that animals and plants, mountains and streams, are inhabited by many spirits or souls. One's deceased ancestors too might roam the locality, and possibly cause problems for the still living.

Shinto, widely practised in Japan, can be considered animistic. It arose out of the nature worship of ancient folk religions.

Religious acts of sacrifice and offering are made to the myriad of mysterious forces that inhabit nature, called kami. Protection is requested, though a more sophisticated interpretation of these rites might be to describe them as tokens of submission to the forces that surround us and that frequently overwhelm us. Shinto practice encourages a befriending of nature, even at its most fierce, and so a reconciliation with life.

To find a way through these questions, we must return to the philosopher who inspired Einstein and whom Dawkins finds almost acceptable. He is Baruch Spinoza, a seventeenth-century Jew of Amsterdam, though he was expelled from his synagogue in 1656, almost certainly because of his controversial religious views.

He came to be known as an atheist, though arguably not in the sense of someone who did not believe in God at all, but in the more common usage, historically speaking, of someone who challenged the conventional notions of God that most held at the time. In this sense, Socrates was called an atheist, though he believed his vocation was inspired by Apollo. The first Christians were called atheists too, because they were not polytheists like the Romans, but monotheists. That said, it could be dangerous to be such an 'atheist'. To be branded a Spinozist was to risk ostracism or punishment right up into the nineteenth century. Spinoza's books were routinely banned until then too.

He seems to have been a warm man whose friendship was valued by those who knew him. In one letter he wrote:

> So far as in me lies, I value, above all other things out of my control, the joining hands of friendship

▲ The friendly face of Baruch Spinoza.

with men who are lovers of truth. I believe that nothing in the world, of things outside our own control, brings more peace than the possibility of affectionate intercourse with such men.

He was a philosopher in the literal sense, a lover of life who quested after truth. The love called friendship that was so central to him fitted with that vocation perfectly, as his friendships were cemented by the affections that arose by sharing the quest. We can add a further dimension to this weave of love and truth. His key work, *The Ethics*, begins with a definition of God and ends with an exploration of God's love. 'Friendship and the pursuit of truth, he believed, contribute to our highest goal – which is amor intellectualis Dei, the intellectual love of God,' explains Roger Scruton in his book *The Great Philosophers: Spinoza*. 'Spinoza's philosophy was an attempt to reconcile this profoundly religious outlook with the scientific view of man,' he adds.

He lived during the period that saw the birth of modern science, as we know it, and saw that the activity called science itself depends upon philosophical assumptions, such as the idea that the cosmos is governed by natural laws. So this raises a major conundrum: why are there natural laws? Indeed, why is there anything at all?

There is no easy way out of this puzzle. Philosophers of all ages have grappled with it. To address the matter head on, and not try to finesse it, Spinoza's opening propositions in his *Ethics* begin with God, by which he means that which exists because it is caused by itself, not by anything else. Only such a being, he implies, can address the issue of why there is something not nothing. Any entity that was not its own cause would require a cause, and then, as the saying goes, you'd have turtles all the way down; you'd be caught up in an infinite regress that captures nothing fundamental.

It is an overtly theological move, coming from another giant of Jewish thought, Moses Maimonides. Similarly, when in his sixth proposition Spinoza comes directly to how to define the concept of God, he deploys terms familiar to philosophical theology.

> *By God, I understand a being absolutely infinite, that is, a substance consisting of infinite attributes, each of which expresses eternal and infinite essence.*

The statement contains an array of difficult technical terms, though might be transcribed in the following way. God is 'distinguished from all lesser things by the completeness and fullness of his being', as Scruton neatly summarizes it. An infinite number of mutually incompatible but equally valid descriptions can be given of God, for all that they will seem to be vastly different. (Strange as that may sound, it is no more peculiar than being able to describe red as an electromagnetic wave of 700 nm length, and red as bright or hot.) By eternity, Spinoza means that God exists outside of time, which is to say that God is a necessary truth, like the proposition that $1 + 1 = 2$.

Working through further implications of these basic suppositions, Spinoza comes to two further conclusions about God, both of which are controversial. First, that God exists by necessity. It is a version of the ontological argument that goes back to Anselm, the intuition that from the conception of an infinite, necessary being, it follows that this being must exist, because not existing would detract from its essence. Further, Spinoza believes that if this intuition is appreciated in all its splendour, then this also implies that everything else that exists exists in God. Everything must be dependent upon the being that is its own cause. Nothing can be that is not in God. And, therefore, everything that is shares in the one being of God.

It is very abstract language and, as a mental aide, the philosopher Clare Carlisle has suggested a helpful metaphor, in an introduction to Spinoza that she wrote for the *Guardian* newspaper:

> *The ocean stands for God, the sole substance, and individual beings are like waves – which are modes of the sea. Each wave has its own shape that it holds for a certain time, but the wave is not separate from the sea and cannot be conceived to exist independently of it. Of course, this is only a metaphor; unlike an infinite God, an ocean has boundaries, and moreover the image of the sea represents God only in the attribute of extension. But maybe we can also imagine the mind of God – that is to say, the infinite totality of thinking – as like the sea, and the thoughts of finite beings as like waves that arise and then pass away.*

It is at this point that it is possible to grasp what is meant when it is said that nature and God are identical. Everything that exists not by its own cause – which is to say, everything that we normally think of as natural, including ourselves – is dependent upon God and is in God. Like a wave rising and falling in harmony or against its neighbours, everything is connected. Further, since Spinoza also argues that only God is truly free, because only God is self-causing, nothing in nature is free, including human beings. It is this kind of argument that caused him so much trouble with his confreres, though Spinoza also thought that there is a kind of freedom human beings can enjoy: using reason, they can contemplate the necessity of nature, and how it could not be other than it is, and this meditation is, imaginatively, to rise above the relentless chain of cause and effect and reflect on matters from the viewpoint of eternity. This is, in fact, the aim of religious and philosophical practice, to alter your perspective to that of God.

Spinoza's contemporaries couldn't stomach it, though, and also seemed to have believed that there was something blasphemous about a philosopher claiming to have proven, and to be able to express, the nature of the divine, as nature. 'The human mind has an adequate knowledge of the eternal and infinite essence of God,' he writes. That said, it is a view of nature that would appeal to science, because that which is not free is determined, and science is in the business of working out just how nature is shaped and governed by laws, which is only possible if the objects of its study are determined like a machine.

So is Spinoza's pantheism really atheism 'sexed up'? There is one aspect of Spinoza's philosophy – one already mentioned – that becomes crucial for those tempted to rush to the conclusion that because Spinoza's God is identical with the natural world, the word 'God' is effectively redundant. Recall that Spinoza argues God has an infinity of attributes, and that this means there are an infinity of mutually incompatible ways of describing divinity. One way will be the way of the natural sciences. For example, if one day physicists derive a 'theory of everything' – a goal which is far from obviously possible – then according to Spinoza's light that would include a complete account of God. But it would not render other accounts of the nature of things, or God, redundant.

A theory of everything would, say, include a scientific theory of sound waves. But that would in no way reduce the absolute importance of the musical appreciation that has nothing to do with physics, and instead addresses the extraordinary experience of listening to the resonance and reverberations that constitute a Beethoven symphony or an owl screeching in the wood.

Similarly, there would still be plenty of work for theologians to do in relation to God. They would have to continue to reflect upon the nature of God, and that would mean they deploy theological language rather than the language of the natural sciences. Never, then, would the language that deploys words such as 'God' be subsumed into the discourse of science. Indeed, if the goal of human life, the nature of our highest freedom, is to gain a God's-eye view of things, 'under the aspect of eternity', as Spinoza puts it, it would appear that theological and philosophical language is absolutely necessary. Science does not strive to comprehend eternity as its modus operandi is intimately and inevitably constrained by the temporal chain of cause and effect. That limitation is both science's great strength and its weakness. 'Things are conceived as actual in two ways', Spinoza explains, 'either in so far as they exist in relation to a certain time and place, or in so far as we conceive them as contained in God, and following from the necessity of the divine nature'.

This explains what Spinoza meant by *amor intellectualis Dei*, the intellectual love of God, and why the expression is not merely a rhetorical flourish but is central to comprehending his way of life. By virtue of human reason, we are able to move in between the realms of humdrum human perspectives and the glorious divine view of all things; from time to timelessness. It is rather like enlarging your vision so that instead of seeing a succession of waves on the surface of the ocean, you gain a view of the ocean as a whole. It is not easy to do. It requires a lifetime of discipline and effort. It is a philosophical way of life to which all aspects of an individual's existence must submit, from their passions to their actions. To achieve it is to be transformed.

Spinoza ends his *Ethics* with a challenge:

> *If the way I have shown to lead to these things now seems very hard, still it can be found. And of course, what is found so rarely must be hard. For if salvation were at hand, and could be found without great effort, how could nearly everyone neglect it? But all things excellent are as difficult as they are rare.*

Spinoza is a pantheist and that sets him against traditional theism. The God of the Hebrew Bible, for example, is distorted by hopeless anthropomorphisms, according to Spinoza. The notion of divine anger, say, is so ridiculous as to almost not be worth discussing amongst philosophers, though it serves a purpose in more everday conversations. He believes that individuals create imaginative fictions to describe the world, collections of stories and impressions that are based upon their personal experience and empirical assumptions. They are, in that way, neither true nor false. They are simply the content of humdrum discourse, and they are very helpful: they can guide us and place our lives within a broader view. The Hebrew Bible is, therefore, not surpassed by Spinoza's philosophy. Religion is a fiction, though not one to discard. Similarly, the Torah is a practical necessity. It always has a place, though the impression he gives is not the supreme place that traditionalists would afford it. Further, people may need prompting to remember that though the stories of God's parting of the Red Sea or distributing manna in the wilderness are tremendous, what they directly imply about God is erroneous, in so far as that is not what God is like in Godself.

At the same time, it is vital to remember that Spinoza's pantheism is not a reduction of God to the frame of the natural sciences. God is everywhere, everything. But God is not one being amongst other beings, because God is self-caused being. Without God there could be no beings, no laws, no world, no science.

Einstein appears to have understood these subtleties. In his biography of the great physicist, *Einstein: His Life and Universe*, Walter Isaacson concludes that Einstein was his own man on the big question of God, as he was on all the others he tackled in his life. His religious sensibility was based upon his appreciation of nature and that 'behind all the discernible laws and connections, there remains something subtle, intangible and inexplicable. Veneration for this force beyond anything that we can comprehend is my religion'. Hence too: 'science without religion is lame, religion without science is blind.' It is a thoroughly Spinozist sentiment: more than one description of the infinity of nature is needed to capture its variety. Similarly with respect to God.

So, too, Einstein used more than one word for God. He often used the word 'Spirit' to refer to this omnipresent force. In one interview, he explicitly said he was not an atheist, adding 'the problem involved is too vast for our limited minds', and on another occasion, 'What separates me from most so-called atheists is a feeling of utter humility toward the unattainable secrets of the harmony of the cosmos'. He appreciated the difficulty of Spinoza's rare pathway to divine understanding.

Similarly, he was a fierce, causal determinist who would not admit of anything like free will. Determinism and God alike were both implicit in his understanding of science – one implies the other – and he drew on the philosophy of Spinoza to make sense of them, also admiring Spinoza's substance monism, as the doctrine that everything is one thing is called. 'Human beings in their thinking, feeling and acting are not free but are as causally bound as the stars in their motions', Einstein thought. Or drawing on Schopenhauer, he agreed that whilst we are free to do what we will, we are not free to will what we will. This is another variation on Spinoza's idea that our freedom comes in contemplating the necessity of the world.

Einstein did differ from Spinoza on some matters. He did not believe in a personal God, in line with the pantheist, but he also did not believe in immortality, though Spinoza did have an account of this. It follows from his aspiration for an intellectual love of God and to see things from the viewpoint of eternity. In so far as this blessed state is possible it moves beyond time, for in reason's purest perceptions there is no past, present or future. Further, this reason exists in human minds. Therefore, there is an aspect of humanity that tastes eternity: 'The human mind cannot be absolutely destroyed with the human body, but something of it remains which is eternal.' It is a flight to a timeless dimension.

Loving or yearning for God – as a philosopher, with philosophical friends – offers salvation, blessedness and liberty. The individual who achieves the intellectual appreciation of God knows God by acquaintance, for this would be 'the very love of God with which God loves himself'. Spinoza's pantheism does not set science and religion against one another in a fight to the death – of theology. Rather, it sets them alongside one another, in the hope that humankind might reach the depths and heights of the divine view.

4

Is God in peak experiences?

During the twentieth century there emerged a distinctive and arguably new conception of how to know God. It is marked by a strong sense of the individual and the individual's capacity for introspection. Instead of turning to theology or philosophy, religious rituals or acts of compassion, it puts its primary emphasis on the psychological. It is the idea that God is to be found in powerful religious experiences – or, to put it another way, the strongest evidence for the existence of God is found in personal, inner experience. Belief in God is fundamentally a subjective stance towards the world, more like trusting than proving.

William James, a founding figure in the modern discipline of psychology, took this felt knowledge of the divine to be the wellspring of spirituality. Religious experiences may be peak experiences. His seminal book, *The Varieties of Religious Experience*, catalogues many such ecstasies. In it, he examines what he takes to be the most valuable material, namely the best articulated and most profound records of conversion.[1] This leaves him open to a charge of religious elitism, as if the 'aficionados' of the spiritual life, as he put it, have the deepest knowledge of God. Countering the charge, he would say that to do otherwise would be like declaring you were going to study music by excluding the work of Bach in favour of nursery rhymes, on the grounds that more people sing *Three Blind Mice* than the St Matthew Passion.

He relates an incident in which a person called Stephen H Bradley attended a revivalist meeting. Later that evening, Bradley was gripped by a powerful sense of God. His heart beat fast. He became elated, while also feeling worthless.

He experienced a stream of air passing through him. The next morning, he believed he could see 'a little heaven upon earth'. He visited his neighbours, 'to converse with [them] on religion, which I could not have been hired to have done before'. He concluded: 'I now defy all the deists and atheists in the world to shake my faith in Christ.'

▲ William James, the genius founder of the modern psychology of religion.

James analysed what had happened in this and countless other cases that result in a sense of regeneration, or a reception of grace or gift of assurance. He concluded that what distinguishes religious conversion from more humdrum experiences of change is depth. Human beings quite normally undergo alterations of character: we are one person at home, another at work, another again when we awake at four in the morning. But religious conversion, be it sudden or slow, results in a transformation that is stable and that causes a revolution in those other parts of our personality. Could this be God?

James resorts to the new language of psychoanalysis, as developed by Sigmund Freud and Carl Jung, and in particular the notion of the unconscious. The point about the unconscious is that it has a life of its own. An individual will never be fully aware, and possibly entirely unaware, of the forces that lurk beneath the waves of their waking lives. Freud tends to have a more pessimistic view of an individual's capacity to tame these troubling influences, proposing that some small degree of understanding, and thereby control, is all that psychoanalysis can aim for. Jung, though, thought that the unconscious could play a redemptive role in life. In its collective manifestations, the unconscious inheritance we share with others is akin to God and may be what theologians call God. Hence, conversion can be thought of as an energetic precipitation from the unconscious and is, generally, for the good. It reorientates the individual around a new centre of previously submerged life.

Religious experiences may, of course, be deluded. Many no doubt are, and require thorough discernment to test their veracity. James himself was also a founding figure in the American philosophical school known as pragmatism. It can be simplified, without doing too much violence to its underlying sophistication, as 'what is true is what works'. James implies that this was an account of truth to be found in the Bible. Take the line, attributed to Jesus, that it is by the fruits of the true disciples that you will know who they are – not, James added, by their roots. What is true cannot be told, it is seen.

Evidence for the human significance and the pragmatic truth of religious experiences is plentiful because so many provide powerful moral inspiration to those who have them. Spiritual boughs are laden with fruit. You might cite the lives of saints who tend to lepers or the dying. You could point to the fact that the majority of charitable organizations were founded by religious people and that the largest network of charitable work in the world today centres on the Roman Catholic church.

James explains how this moral 'genius' gains its strength. Religious experiences, he said, have a unique ability to overcome the inhibitions that usually prevent people from behaving in morally exemplary ways: 'Few people who have not expressly reflected on the matter realise how constantly this factor of inhibition is upon us, how it contains and moulds us by its restrictive pressure almost as if we were fluids pent within the cavity of a jar.' The inhibition that makes us turn away from the wayfarer asking for money on the street, and that keeps us preoccupied when all around there is suffering, is largely an unconscious force. Hence counterbalancing unconscious forces, such as those that are spiritual, are required to release the individual from the impulses that hold them back from compassion and good works. 'Magnanimities once impossible are now easy' for the religious, James explains.

Dark night of the soul

Many of the religious experiences James discusses were felt as positive. But he was more than aware that the 'more', as he sometimes referred to God, may also be discovered through painful, disturbing and depressive episodes.

He was himself prone to this bleaker route. In *The Varieties of Religious Experience* he describes an incident supposedly told to him by a 'French correspondent', though he later admitted that this individual was himself. He tells of being in a melancholic frame of mind, and then suddenly falling into a spiritual crisis one evening. Walking into his dressing room, 'there fell upon me without any warning, just as if it came out of darkness, a horrible fear of my own existence'.

Then came a vision of 'an epileptic patient whom I had seen in the asylum, a black-haired youth with greenish skin, entirely idiotic'. He fears he will become that poor soul. Feeling out of control, 'I became a mass of quivering fear', a nauseating sense that stayed close to him for months. He finds some comfort and refuge in citing texts of scripture. Phrases such as 'the eternal God is my refuge' and 'I am the resurrection and the life' echo around his mind. It is not that he believed them in any straightforward sense: James remained close to agnosticism for much of his life. Rather, they helped him feel a way through the crisis to a place of hope, as if the doctrinal statements functioned like poetic windows on a deeper, trustworthy reality.

Any discussion of religious experiences, particularly if asking whether they provide evidence for God, requires a consideration of mystical experiences and mysticism. James agreed. 'One may say truly, I think, that personal religious experience has its roots and centre in mystical states of consciousness,' he writes.

That said, it's important to be clear about what he means by phrases like 'states of consciousness'. Today, such a view is coloured by the psychologizing tendency that has only grown stronger since James's time. That development can be associated, in particular, with a schema proposed by the humanistic psychologist, Abraham Maslow. He describes 'peak experiences' as the ecstatic states that satisfy the highest human need for self-actualization, but this exaltation of feelings of interconnectedness is questionable on two counts.

First, Maslow's analysis is scientifically dubious. In their book *Selling Spirituality*, Jeremy Carrette and Richard King explain that 'sampling disillusioned college graduates, Maslow would ask his interviewees about their ecstatic and rapturous moments in life'. To put it crudely, it is worth reflecting on whether or not students provide the best samples of mystics. A second critique of Maslow's work is found in the writings of the greatest spiritual practitioners. The anonymous author of *The Cloud of Unknowing*, for one, explicitly argues that, whatever the mystical might be, it is hidden from experience. Or, as any thoughtful meditation teacher will tell you, clinging to oceanic experiences will hinder your progress quite as much as clinging to anything else.

This is not to say that mystical experience has nothing to do with feelings, James continues. Rather, it is a state of both feeling and knowledge, of both wonder and intellectual

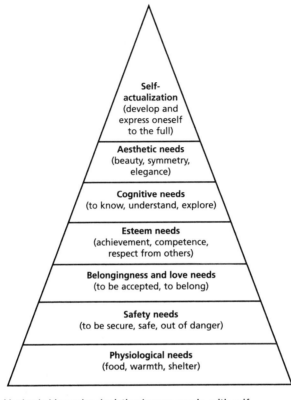

▲ Maslow's hierarchy, depicting human needs, with self-actualization at the top.

engagement. All the faculties must be deployed when weighing any insight. 'What comes,' James explains, 'must be sifted and tested, and run the gauntlet of confrontation with the total context of experience'. Mystical states can, therefore, be assessed for their truth value. But how?

Not, James explains, in the way advocated by what he called 'medical materialism'. Medical materialism notes that religious experiences have a biological substrate, say in unique brain states observable now in brain scanners. It therefore concludes that the experiences can be wholly explained by such brain states, as if they were nothing more than brain states. This is a mistake. We are psychosomatic creatures. What is of significance for us psychologically or spiritually is bound to have physical correlates. But observing behaviour or effects associated with the latter does not mean that the meaning of the former has been understood.

This 'too simple-minded system . . . finishes up Saint Paul by calling his vision on the road to Damascus a discharging lesion of the occipital cortex, he being an epileptic. It snuffs out Saint Teresa as an hysteric', James wrote. Similarly, mystic experiences cannot be reduced, as was suggested in his time, to 'hypnoid states, on an intellectual basis of superstition, and a corporeal one of degeneration and hysteria'. After all, he remarks,

> scientific theories are organically conditioned just as much as religious emotions are; and if we only knew the facts intimately enough, we should doubtless see 'the liver' determining the dicta of the sturdy atheist as decisively as it does those of the Methodist under conviction anxious about his soul.

In effect, if you explain religious experience as nothing more than biological phenomena, then you evacuate the truth content of all utterances made by human beings.

The scientific study of religion

Today, it is quite common to assume that the scientific study of religion can not only contribute to understanding humanity's spiritual side but will do away with it, perhaps by showing that religiosity is an excess of human feeling that belongs to former, more superstitious times.

William James was profoundly sceptical of this view. He proposed a number of reasons for this, the most obvious found in the very title of his lectures. Religious experience is marked by its 'varieties'. It is nothing if not multiple and various.

Hence, any single explanation of religion will struggle with the variety. Scientific theories tend to need to reduce the object of their study to identifiable, discrete parts. In the case of religion, a common assumption is that its essence lies in the tendency to ascribe spiritual agency to inanimate forces, say as a by-product of evolution. But such approaches always leave too much out, and the evidence is often forced to fit the prior assertions.

Better, then, to see the psychology of religion as a taxonomical endeavour, one which attempts to sift the variety and categorize, as James did.

More controversially, James also believes that the truth of mystical experience has little to do with the specificities of the times and places in which they occurred – which puts him at odds with scholars today, who generally emphasize the opposite – the need for a dialogue between any particular experience and its historical context. For example, the Jewish scholar

Gershom Scholem coined the term 'historiosophy' to capture the mixture of real-life events and metaphysical responses that he argued was implicit in mystical experience. A case in point is the origins of Lurianic Kabbala, which Scholem interpreted as a reaction to the expulsion of the Jews from Spain in 1492.

James, though, is mostly interested in the individual, not communal, significance of mysticism and, further, he inclines to the view that it is real and positive. 'In mystic states', he writes, 'we both become one with the Absolute and we become aware of our oneness'. In short, there are two characteristic outcomes: optimism and monism. This, he believes, is amply demonstrated in copious accounts of mystical experience. Generally speaking, the religious move 'from a less into a more, as from a smallness into a vastness, and at the same time as from an unrest to a rest. We feel them as reconciling, unifying states'.

Again, such perspectival shifts could be deluded. The experience may be 'nothing but [a] subjective way of feeling things, a mood of . . . fancy'. James also considers what he calls 'lower mysticisms', a category that includes states of consciousness that are the product of chemical not spiritual stimulation. An example is alcohol: 'The sway of alcohol over mankind is unquestionably due to its power to stimulate the mystical faculties of human nature, usually crushed to earth by the cold facts and dry criticisms of the sober hour.'

Nonetheless, there is, for James, such a thing as genuine mystical experience, providing a pointer to a reality that is more likely true than false. The sense of oneness and the psychological optimism that they bestow have such a demonstrably positive impact upon the lives of those who have them.

He wants to stress that a felt experience is necessary for a truly vibrant spiritual life. He loathes what he elsewhere calls 'vicious intellectualism', the preference for intellectual concepts to the detriment of emotional reality. It is cultivated by the fantasy of an objective science and is insidious because it turns you into a cool spectator of life, rather than an active participant. It encourages speculation for speculation's sake, and, like bankers who engage in the financial equivalent, the result is ideological bubbles. They rise high in the intellectual firmament before they burst and crash back to earth, forcing everyone back to square one. In the sphere of religion, James detects such vicious intellectualism most clearly in the attempts to demonstrate the existence of God as an a priori fact. The ontological and cosmological proofs are for those who wish to cleanse themselves of the 'muddiness and accidentality' of the real world, he fears.

Interestingly, he describes John Henry Newman as one such 'vexed spirit'. He charges the saint and cardinal with a 'disdain for sentiment', though that seems unfair. Newman seems quite close to James in certain respects, particularly in relation to what Newman called the 'grammar of assent'.

Newman makes a crucial distinction between 'notional assent' and 'real assent'. To determine a belief using your philosophical head alone is to give notional assent. But when it comes to religious questions, that is an inadequate way to proceed because it engages only the rational part. Real assent requires more, Newman argues. It is a convergence of the full assortment of evidences and experiences we have – rational, emotional, observational and cultural. Each in itself may not be wholly compelling. But, added together, they support a belief that powerfully rings true. Newman likens it to a cable: a single strand is easily broken. But wound together, strands form a cable that is strong. So, real assent implies that God is not a hypothesis. Rather, belief in God is 'an action more subtle and more comprehensive than the mere appreciation of syllogistic logic', Newman wrote.

This chimes well with the conclusions James draws in his essay, 'The Will to Believe', published a few years before *The Varieties*. It is a thoroughly misleading title, as the idea that you can will belief in God is 'simply silly', James observes. Rather, the essay seeks to justify the beliefs individuals have 'in spite of the fact that our merely logical intellect may not have been coerced'. It could be said to be an essay about real assent.

James starts by defining religious beliefs. To count as such, they are not abstract propositions but must be living and genuine options for the individual concerned, which is to say that they appeal to and are real possibilities for him or her to adopt. For a western agnostic, Christianity would be a living, genuine option, in a way that belief in the Egyptian sun god Ra could never be. Religious beliefs are also momentous, which is to say that should one be gripped by what they represent, it would change one's outlook on life.

In 'The Will to Believe', James references Pascal's wager, the argument that belief in God is rational because, if true, the believer stands to make an infinite gain and, if false, nothing much is lost. James sees the wager for what it is, of course: the logic of 'the gaming table', as he describes it. But he is curious enough to wonder why a brilliant man like Pascal penned such an argument. He concludes that it made sense to the French philosopher and mathematician, in spite of the obvious objections, because Christianity had a genuine and momentous allure for Pascal. Fundamentally, it addressed his soul.

Seen in that light, the wager works like this. The panoply of Pascal's experiences and convictions were drawing him towards Christianity. But that weight of evidence 'ran before' his rational mind, because Christianity demands real not notional assent. Moreover, as 'the mere appreciation of syllogistic logic' cannot of itself decide the case, the wager was never meant to stand alone. It was originally just a note in a private commonplace book. What the wager represents is Pascal justifying his religious intuitions to his mathematical mind. It is one strand in the cable of his belief. Understand the wager in this way, James concludes, and 'instead of being powerless, [it] seems like a regular clincher'. It worked for Pascal. It might for others. But it is never going to work for everyone. It didn't work for James. But, nonetheless, he respected Pascal's attempt to integrate his whole person into his desire – his will – to believe.

More generally, then, there will never be a universal, objective proof for or against God. Instead, there will be multiple, plural strands that work for individuals and groups when incorporated into their real assent. This is the way to understand the evidence provided by the remarkable experiences that people have of the more, of God. They stand out because they are exceptional and compelling. They change lives because they allow the individual to return to life renewed. That is the work of God.

5

How can we say God is good?

It might be thought that goodness is to God as brightness is to light. One almost automatically implies the other. What else might God be, if God were not all good? What else might we mean when we describe someone as a 'godly person', if not a good person? So it is striking that when theologians such as Thomas Aquinas have asked what is meant by the phrase 'God is good', they have insisted that God's goodness is not like human goodness at all.

God is not morally good, say, as if God were good to know, or always behaved in a good way, or were virtuous, or had integrity. God is not a good person either, because a person is a creature with a mind that changes many times a day and God cannot be like that. Also, Aquinas notes, the Bible never refers to God as a person. It only relatively rarely refers to God as good too, for that matter, though God is more commonly said to do good things.

Euthyphro's dilemma

One of the most common arguments that does the rounds in debates about the existence of God originates in a dialogue of Plato, called the Euthyphro. In it, Socrates bumps into a man called Euthyphro, who was known to be something of a religious expert. They embark upon a conversation that tries to define what is pious, or good.

The crux of the discussion might be summarized as whether something is pious or good because God decrees it, or whether something is pious or good because it is pious or good in itself. If the latter obtains then this seems to suggest that God is subject to what is set as good regardless of what God desires. That, in turn, seems to set a limit on God's power, as if God were subject to some higher law that determines goodness.

Socrates and Euthyphro don't actually reach any settled conclusion. They find it too hard to define 'good' or 'God'. Rather, they end by recognizing that the matter is far more subtle than they first presumed and they are not sure just what they are talking about. However, in modern atheism debates, the dialogue is used to drive a cleaver between God and morality, as if godliness has nothing intrinsically to do with goodness, and then further, as if religion has nothing intrinsically to do with morality. We won't pick up that argument here, but simply note that theologians like Aquinas would be more inclined to follow the implication of Plato's dialogue. Just what we might mean when we use the words 'God' and 'goodness' in the same sentence is, literally speaking, well nigh impossible to say.

Aquinas has precise reasons for this caution. For one thing, he asks what is meant by saying something is good. He believes that good is a relative term, by which is meant that it qualifies something to which it refers. 'Good' is therefore like 'hot' or 'fast', not like 'square' or 'blue'. If I say the field is square or the sky is blue then those observations make sense in themselves. But if I say the weather is hot or the car is fast then that raises the questions, hotter than when and faster than what? Weather that is hot for the Arctic would be cold for the Sahara. A fast domestic car would be last off the grid in a Formula One race.

Similarly, a fast car might be referred to as a good car, or hot weather as good weather. But to make sense when doing so, you first have to know quite a lot about cars and the weather. And that kind of information is not available to us when we talk about God. Aquinas argues that even if we are sure that God exists, it is not possible to be sure what God is. This simply follows from the concept of God. God cannot be another thing that exists in the cosmos, because God is the reason there is a cosmos, and so somehow stands above and before everything else. Put it this way: when you set out to define the subject of physics, you can determine both what you are studying and how you will study it. Physics is about the natural world and you can study it by examining the fundamental constituents of nature. However, theology is not so transparent. You can say theology is about God. But beyond that, it is hard to say because God is, by definition, not just difficult to study – which physics is too – but is beyond direct observation, which the natural world is not. Hence, Aquinas concludes: 'Whatever way we have of thinking of him is a way of failing to understand him as he really is.'

But all is not lost. There is another way forward. It is called the negative way, or apophatic theology. Aquinas describes it like this: 'Now we cannot know what God is, but only what he is not; we must therefore consider the ways in which God does not exist, rather than the ways in which he does.'

▲ The unknown divine is often depicted in art as cloud or the sun marked by the tetragrammaton, or four-letter name of God.

Apophatic theology, or the negative way

The negative way, or apophatic theology, says that God is ineffable, that is beyond telling: all talk of God falls short. It was taken as read for millennia, but in the modern world, inspired by the successes of science, such theology has, arguably, become unfashionable and even a source of annoyance.

In fact, divine ineffability can be interpreted as a form of pseudo-profundity, a form of theological bullshit. For example, in *Humanism: A Very Short Introduction*, Stephen Law writes: 'The view that we cannot say what God is, only what God is not . . . has its attractions, perhaps the most obvious being that, if you never say what God is, you can never be contradicted.' Touché. The fear is that appealing to a mystery or the unknown is not done out of intellectually necessity, as Aquinas and others argued, but is resorted to simply to throw smokescreens around the credulous.

Pseudo-profundity is always a risk. Religious language has to operate at the limits of reason and sense, and so discernment is a critical task in matters theological and spiritual. But I suspect that what lies underneath the fear of bullshit is a deeper fear about the nature of reason.

Reason, if you like, cannot pull itself up by its own bootstraps. It needs an intuition – something pre-rational – to get itself going, to get its teeth into. In other words, it has a subsidiary role to experience, inklings, encounters, hunches – the full panoply of ways in which we engage with the world and God. When it comes to God, I suspect that this is why few people reason their way into belief or non-belief. Rather, it is experience that does most of the work, which is then honed by reason.

The conclusion would be that it seems inevitable that pseudo-profundity will always be with us, and it's well worth living with because life for we humans is just more than we can grasp. Better some bullshit than denying all our most profound intuitions. Our sure knowledge will always rest on a sea of unknowing.

An analogy might be useful. Imagine you have lived all your life in a landlocked country, where there is no talk or sight, let alone comprehension, of the sea. There is not even the word. Then, one day, you venture across the horizon and after a long journey reach the end of land. And you see it: the sea. Astonished, you contemplate the view for a while and then you head back to your fellows. You try to describe what you've seen, though you're not even sure yourself. It's not land, you begin. It's not hilly or mountainous, you continue. It's not possible to walk across it. It's not covered with grass and trees. It's a bit like that lake, only it has no apparent bounds and it does weird things like approaching the land and then retreating from it, day by day.

You take the point. Quite a lot can be said negatively, by saying it's not like what the landlocked peers are familiar with and by using some analogies with a negative twist. Similarly, as Aquinas says of God, it's not that mere mortals can have no knowledge of God, but because by definition what God truly would be lies beyond the comprehension of finite, mortal beings, the most certain knowledge will be found by saying what God is not.

A simple example is the statement that God is invisible, which simply means not visible. Nothing positive is contained in that description. Similarly, God cannot be mortal, which is why believers often call God immortal. That does not affirm anything positive about God. What it does suggest, though, is that to be mortal would be to cease to exist, and if that were true of God, then that would mean God was sometimes not all that God might be, which would be an odd belief to have about a supreme deity. In general that also means that theology will always be provisional and hedged with mystery. (Incidentally, the Christian via negativa has parallels in many other religious traditions too. In the Upanishads of the Indian tradition, from around 600 BCE, a description of the Absolute is requested. The text replies, 'It's not like this, it's not like that.')

We are in a position to understand why Aquinas does not believe that God's goodness can be described as a form of moral goodness. Moral qualities, such as being just or truthful, do make some sense when applied to God: whatever God might be, it should be said, God must be at least as just or truthful as the best human beings. The problem with that, though, is that it also carries the implication that many human beings are not just or truthful. Failure is part of what we are referring to when we talk of moral qualities. God cannot be a moral failure, and so must be 'above morality', or 'beyond good and evil' to deploy Nietzsche's phrase. To put it more precisely, God transcends moral virtues, in an equal and opposite way that a mountain, or the wasp that lays its eggs in live caterpillars from which its young then feed, cannot be said to be moral entities either.

So much for the inbuilt failure of talk about God. But there is a different sense in which we may say God is good, to which we can now turn. In many of his reflections, Aquinas takes a lead from the ancient Greek philosopher Aristotle. It was Aquinas who almost single-handedly knitted Aristotelian philosophy with Christian theology, when the works of 'the philosopher', as Aquinas referred to him, reappeared in the west in the

▲ William Blake's image of God as The Ancient of Days is a satire. Blake thought that imagining God as a divine designer was laughable.

twelfth century. When it comes to goodness, Aristotle notes that 'good is well defined by those who say it is what everything desires' or, more succinctly, good is 'that at which all things aim'. What he means is that whatever is good for an oak, say, or a cow is what that oak or cow will seek out – for all that they may have no conscious conception of what it is that they desire. The oak reaches for the sun, with no understanding of light. The cow munches grass and laboriously chews the cud, with no real understanding of how difficult it is to digest its staple diet. They do, though, desire what is good for them. The oak does seek the sun; the cow fresh pasture. So, it can be said that without knowledge of what is good, they are no less compelled towards it.

We can generalize the point. What is good for creatures is what enables them to become all that they might be. Conversely, what is bad are impediments to that realization. To use Aquinas's language, the good is that which actualizes everything that is otherwise only potentially so. The oak can grow into a mighty tree with the light. The cow can produce milk. To be good is to be something and to have achieved a degree of perfection that is appropriate to that something. Further, achieving that goal is supremely desirable for the creature because the good represents its best flourishing.

Returning to God's goodness, this means we can say something positive about what we mean by it, aside from the restrictions imposed by the necessity of the negative way. For Aquinas, the monotheist, God is the supreme goal of what all creatures desire. This is a different sense in which God can be said to be good. God is the good goal for which all created things yearn.

Different creatures will show their tendency towards God differently, and it is fair to conclude that only human beings will struggle to articulate how. However, nature's grandeur, to recall Charles Darwin's observation about the 'endless forms most beautiful and most wonderful', speaks of the glory of God because its vibrancy, complexity and sheer striving tells of the drive for life, which is the cumulated drive to become all that earth's creatures might be. Indeed, in the light of contemporary knowledge of evolution, life not only drives for all it might be, but for all that it will be too. Aquinas puts it this way:

> Now created things must all fall short of the full goodness of God, so, in order that things may reflect that goodness more perfectly, there had to be variety in things, so that what one thing couldn't express perfectly could be more perfectly expressed in various ways by a variety of things. For human beings too, when they can't express the idea in their minds in one word, resort to many different ones that express the idea in different ways. And this also draws attention to how great God's perfection is: for the perfect goodness that exists one and unbroken in God can exist in creatures only in a multitude of fragmented ways.

In a different place, Aquinas deploys the metaphor of radiance to describe the goodness of God. The notion of radiance appeals for two reasons. First, it is active, emanating from a body like light from the sun. Similarly, God's goodness draws us to itself, both because it is our ultimate desire – even for individuals who do not believe in God, Aquinas argued – and because its warmth reaches down to us. Second, radiance appeals because it does not compel. It offers an attractive goal to which the individual can strive, can set his or her life towards.

But the individual is still free to choose a different goal in life, another orientation. It will be less good, according to the believer, because if the individual struggles to that end – perhaps the accumulation of money or fame – they will not become all they might be. In such cases, Aquinas believes that reason and example, or perhaps a personal crisis or disaster, are required to persuade an individual that they have set their course by the wrong chart, and that God's goodness offers a better aim.

It might be asked how we can aim at the goodness God intends, if we only know God negatively, if we know it at all. The relationship between a mother and child, as described in psychoanalysis, may offer a useful analogy. Take the work of the British psychotherapist W R Bion. He offers an account of how the quest for what is good for the baby emerges from the mother's ability to empathize with her infant in a particular way. The young child will have all manner of experiences as part of the turbulence of its ordinary life, from states of complete satisfaction, perhaps during a feed, to frightening moments of terror when it feels threatened or as if it is falling apart – as the adult may later put it, unconsciously recalling the infantile experience. Bion argued that a mother can teach her child to bear these experiences by emotionally engaging with them herself. She does this in the way that she cradles her child, responds to its gaze, meets its demands. It is an art, not a science, because she has to do it in such a way that the baby, over time, feels that the blissful gratification or the sheer panic can be understood not in a cognitive way, but emotionally or imaginatively.

Bion called it reverie, an engagement with an experience of distress that, whilst ensuring it does not overcome the child, nonetheless does not attempt to explain it, which the child will not understand. Instead, reverie stays with it. This allows the child to see it for what it is too. His or her experiences then stop being random and disconnected, that arbitrarily and alarmingly appear to come and go, and start to be recognized as part of an overall pattern of life. Some moments will be unsettling and frightening. But the child who has seen its mother feeling her way through them with it will learn to place them in a wider context too, thereby organizing them and rendering them meaningful. He or she can then become a person too, with a developing inner sense of what is good for it, known as much in the body as the mind, searched for by feelings and intuitions, rather than foreknowledge. When this reciprocity goes right, Bion describes the baby as gaining a sense of beauty and truthfulness, resting on the goodness to which its instincts are aimed.

William Wordsworth recalled this early growing experience towards what is good in his poem 'The Prelude'. He describes how the child 'with his soul/Drinks in the feelings of his Mother's eye!', and writes:

> *For him, in one dear Presence, there exists*
> *A virtue which irradiates and exalts*
> *Objects through widest intercourse of sense.*
> *No outcast he, bewildered and depressed.*

By analogy, then, God's goodness may be said to touch the unknowing souls of God's creatures and, by its reverie and radiance, speak to the deepest needs and longings of humankind. Paradoxically, we do not need to know about God's goodness to sense that we need God's goodness. Like a mother's eye for the unknowing infant, it is that to which all of God's creation strives.

6

Is God green?

A giant statue of Lao Tzu commands the skyline as one approaches Maoshan monastery, about 60 kilometres from Nanjing. He appears to sit on the sacred buildings as if they were his throne. It is a recent construction, and beneath him is a plaque that declares the master of Taoism, God of Ecological Protection. Lao Tzu holds a beehive, which government officials requested to be removed. The monks refused, saying that they cannot interfere with nature. It remains.

Here is another vignette from modern China. The Chinese Taoist Association, a division of the government's Religious Affairs Bureau, recently issued a statement on global ecology: 'We believe that as the Chinese state and society today are paying greater attention to ecological problems, educational programs concerning public health issues will be further fostered and developed.'

The stories are telling of the revival of Taoism in China and of Taoism's increasing role in engaging with growing environmental concerns. Further, as Taoist expert Martin Palmer told me, there is another dimension at play here. Taoism is not a monotheistic religion: it deliberately stands apart from the dramatic growth of faiths such as Christianity coming from the west. That debate about the role of religions, imported and indigenous, can be put alongside the ecological concerns and from it rises a central theological question that we will now consider: whether so-called polytheistic beliefs conceal a one, high divinity behind their multifaceted theologies.

Palmer explains that there has long been a tension between plural and monotheist world religions. (In fact, referring to non-monotheistic beliefs as 'polytheistic' is now seen as pejorative.) Broadly speaking, the tendency is for polytheism to be viewed as more primitive, with monotheism as more advanced, intellectually and culturally. The elite claim is built on monotheism's association with colonial powers and conquest, and more developed societies. But now, climate change is providing plural religions with a chance to fight back.

The many divinities of Hinduism

Pressure on native polytheism was felt by what is now called Hinduism – the collection of indigenous religions of India – when the subcontinent felt the impact of monotheistic Islam, about a millennium ago. A tendency emerged to consolidate the many divinities of the tradition into a trinity of the gods Brahma, Vishnu and Shiva. Referred to as the Trimurti, the three can be viewed as personifications of the cosmic realities of creativity, sustenance and destruction, respectively. They are taken to be the central manifestations of the invisible godhead, a theology that sat more comfortably with Islam's acceptance of non-Muslim monotheisms, and more aggressive attitudes towards polytheism.

The birth of Sikhism in the sixteenth century marks another milestone in this story. Sikhism is strictly monotheistic, the first indigenous Indian religion to be so.

Taoism suffered massively under the communist regime of Mao Zedong in the mid-twentieth century. It has been estimated that 98 per cent of Taoist temples and buildings were either demolished or reappropriated, with 97 per cent of Taoist texts and other religious paraphernalia being destroyed too. Monotheism played an indirect part in this oppression in as much as Marxist philosophy can be called a child of the monotheistic worldview. To put it simply, both are monolithic.

Marx himself argued that religion should be allowed to wither on the vine. He believed that as people's material conditions improved, religious faith would have less and less of a grip on the human imagination. However, monotheism encourages uniform political aspirations. Sometimes these are benign, such as the inspiration that can link monotheism and the concept of a brother- and sisterhood of all humankind: if everyone is under one God, then everyone is one. But at other times, monolithic aspirations are malign, and Taoism suffered particularly because it was designated a superstition. It was respected even less than Christianity and Confucianism because, as a plural religion, it had no single, rationally defendable philosophy.

It suffered another blow because its many gods, parading in a celestial court, were modelled on the earthly court of the pre-communist royal hierarchies. With the imperial city swept away, an important element in the Taoist imagination was left floundering too.

But then, in the 1980s, there was a remarkable turnaround in this decline. Religious organizations were authorized and practices once again sanctioned. The Chinese government also sponsored the academic study of religion. Evidence of the standing Taoism had regained emerged when, in 2011, and for the first time in nearly 900 years, the Chinese government asked Taoist scholars for advice on how to manage the country. The last time this happened was in 1219, when Genghis Khan summoned Taoist Master Qiu Chuji to come to his war camp in the Himalayas and advise him on his plans to conquer China. This time it even featured a nationwide, televised debate.

Falun Gong

The only Taoist-related sect that has not benefited from the recent revival of religion in China is the Falun Gong movement. It is a synthesis of Buddhism and Taoist Qigong techniques, meaning 'energy control', a collection of meditations, breathing exercises and dietary rules aimed at lengthening life, a perennial concern in Taoism. Falun Gong has fallen foul of the government's phobia of millenarianism – eschatological hopes that feature in Falun Gong – and which have caused successive Chinese administrations trouble in the past.

Today, Palmer continues to explain, Taoism is rebuilding itself with a reduced portfolio of deities. Particularly under threat are the military deities of yesteryear's warring states and the local deities of particular districts and mountains. Conversely, the deities that are thriving are those that can be associated with the new way of life that many Chinese are now enjoying under capitalism. Gods of wealth, health, longevity, childbirth and academic success do well in the rebuilt and reopened temples.

There is another side to Taoism that is also growing in strength. It is quietly critical of unbridled capitalism, and it is here that Taoism's ecological credentials can be seen. The abbot of Maoshan monastery put it this way, in an interview with Tim Gardam for the BBC:

> We Taoists also speak of an order in the way of dealing with things. For example, water from the mountains will flow downwards. You shouldn't fight against it. We also speak of a carefree and unfettered life. That is what we need in Chinese society right now. If you have money, what happens? You'll be ill at ease in your soul. If you have power, what happens? You'll find it a real headache. But in Taoism what is important is being a healthy, happy person. So lots of things in Taoism are good for society.

Taoism can be divided into two broad, but intertwined, traditions. The first is philosophical Taoism, a considered and careful way of life, which originated first around 500 BCE with the thinkers Lao Tzu and Chuang Tzu. The second is religious Taoism, which grew from the revelations of Zhang Ling in the second century CE and is regarded as an incarnation of the Tao, the principle upon which the existence of the cosmos and all things rests. A fully fledged system of rituals, doctrines and superstitions, religious Taoism promises final ascent to be with the immortals. Trying to summarize millennia-old paths of thought and practice is, of course, a mug's game. However, the ecological dimension with Taoism might be described in this way.

One of the core teachings is that 'the Tao that can be talked about is not the true Tao'. Quite what is meant by this phrase deliberately cannot be pinned down. It is the kind of gnomic injunction that is designed to show rather than tell, to precipitate insight rather than fall for the delusions of succinct explanations. But some indications as to the character of the Way of Nature, the Tao, can be offered.

In his translation of *The Book of Chuang Tzu*, Palmer indicates what might be meant by the Tao by describing it as 'the Way of Nature which, if you could become part of it, would carry you in its flow to the edge of reality and beyond, into the world of nature'.

How that might be so could be represented in the personal freedom that Chuang Tzu is said to have enjoyed, particularly in relation to the ways in which human civilization inevitably binds and enslaves the human spirit, for all else that it brings. This liberal spirit is well captured, Palmer says, in the stories about how he resisted the trappings of power. He was offered a post at court, to which in one version of the story he replied, 'Go away! Don't mess with me! I would rather enjoy myself in the mud than be a slave to the ruler of some kingdom. I shall never accept such an office, and so I shall remain free to do as I will.' There are many more of this kind of retort. Palmer notes that *The Book of Chuang Tzu* contains a 'trail of humour, bruised egos and damaged reputations'.

A variation on the theme comes when babies are cited as being knowledgeable about the Tao. Lao Tzu is reported to have said:

> The baby cries all day long but its throat never becomes hoarse: that indeed is perfect harmony. The baby clenches its fist all day long but never

gets cramp, it holds fast to Virtue. The baby stares
all day long but it is not affected by what is outside
it. It moves without knowing where, it sits without
knowing where it is sitting, it is quietly placid and
rides the flow of events. This is how to protect life.

Chuang Tzu's record is written as a kind of travelogue, not a systematic exploration of concepts. 'A narrow-minded scholar cannot discuss the Tao because he is constrained by his teachings', the god of the North Ocean, Jo, remarks at another point. If the Tao is the Way of Nature, it is experienced only by undertaking an often painful way or path. Certainties must be given up because the invariably futile attempt to hold onto them only provokes anxieties and doubts and masks what is innate and true.

The opposition between civilization and nature – enjoy the mud rather than be slave to a kingdom – is just one example of that trope. Similarly, there is divined an opposition between what can be called innate or true nature and the artifices of civilized life. Chapter 9 of *The Book of Chuang Tzu* contains the following:

The potter said, 'I know how to use clay, how to mould
it into rounds like the compass and into squares as
though I had used a T-square.' The carpenter said,
'I know how to use wood: to make it bend, I use the
template; to make it straight, I use the plumb line.'
However, is it really the innate nature of clay and
wood to be moulded by compass and T-square,
template and plumb line? It is true, nevertheless,
that generation after generation has said, 'Po Lo [a

famous horse trainer] is good at controlling horses, and indeed the potter and carpenter are good with clay and wood.' And the same nonsense is spouted by those who rule the world.

The ragbag quality of Chuang Tzu's teachings, which stumble and fall over themselves, is also opposed to any tight logic or reasoning. The Tao that can be talked about is not the true Tao.

Another aspect of Taoism with ecological importance is that of wuwei, or non-assertive action. It is a cautious approach to making interventions in nature and plays well in ecological strategies because the environment is a complex system: it is often far from clear what effects an action in one area will have on another. The Taoist scholar, Liu Xiaogan, writes: 'Environmental preservation involves serious and complicated issues affecting various groups of people, different nations and regions; thus it demands a patient, gradual and enduring working attitude that is in line with the Taoist wisdom of wuwei.' The point is that problems as complicated as climate change are not solved by global, monolithic solutions but require detailed granular knowledge that respects local principles and values.

A further resource in Taoism has been highlighted by another scholar, James Miller. In an article entitled 'Envisioning the Taoist Body', he notes how Taoism maps the world in the human body and the human body in the world. The two are seen to be intimately related so that 'we human beings are inextricably woven into the fabric of our natural environment'. Miller continues:

In one sense, therefore, the mystical aspect of the Daoist religion may be considered as comprising ways to realize 'the whole glory' of the unity of humans, heaven, and earth. The organic metaphors employed in Daoist writing suggest that this unity is to be conceived as an ontogenetic unity, that is, a root from which the diversity of things flowers. The genetic metaphor of root and branch (ben-mo) is a powerful way of conceiving our relation to the primordial source (yuandao) from which all life flows. Human beings experience a unity with this transformative, multifarious vitality within their bodies.

▲ Earth from space, our island home.

Taoism resists anthropocentrism. This is also made clear in a story, told in another Taoist text, the Lieh Tzu.

It concerns a man who prepares a feast for his friends. Casting an eye at the banquet he has ordered, he praises the heavens for its kindness to humanity, copiously providing all manner of grains, fish and birds. But a 12-year-old boy pipes up in protest:

> My Lord is wrong! All life is born in the same way that we are and we are all of the same kind. One species is not nobler than another; it is simply that the strongest and cleverest rule over the weaker and more stupid. Things eat each other and are eaten, but they were not bred for this. To be sure, we can take the things which we eat and consume them, but you cannot claim that Heaven made them in the first place just for us to eat. After all, mosquitoes and gnats bite our skin, tigers and wolves eat our flesh. Does this mean Heaven originally created us for the sake of mosquitoes, gnats, tigers and wolves?

Palmer describes this as 'the authentic voice of the Taoist. Here is the debunking of human pretensions and the re-assertion of the natural as the highest order'.

Christian ecotheology

Western Christianity has traditionally envisaged humankind as at the pinnacle of the created order. It is known as the doctrine of the imago dei, the anthropology that understands individuals to be made in the image of God. There are benign aspects to this: the imago dei played a key conceptual role in the development of human rights. But the malign aspects are played out in the creation theology that imagines God gave human beings command over nature, the world becoming little more than a resource for human beings to explore and exploit.

The Elizabethan politician and philosopher, Francis Bacon, can be cited here, a man whose philosophy of knowledge-as-power laid the foundations for modern science. Nature not only could but should be exploited, he argued. This is humankind's God-given destiny. Nature can be tortured in order that she reveal her secrets.

The effort to develop an ecotheology in Christianity is, therefore, often focused on highlighting those passages in the Bible that stress the careful stewardship of creation. Consider, for example, the remark that follows God's creation of the natural world, though, before the sixth day when God finally creates human beings: 'And God saw that it was good.' Nature is good in itself, before the existence of humankind. Humankind should, therefore, respect nature as a good in itself.

Religious Taoism, it might be said, provides a place for the new gods of consumerism. Philosophical Taoism, instead, contemplates the order of nature. The goal is to evolve into harmony with its hidden ways. 'Taoism is saying', Palmer explains, 'that non-theism and many deities serve modern people better'. Such a worldview reverses monotheistic traditions, which tend to view humankind's task as to be managers or users of nature, as God's representatives on earth. Instead, Taoism recognizes that the metaphor of managing nature already creates a sense of separation from nature and is, further, deluded. It is not that we protect the forests; the forests protect us.

What these reflections amount to is that the emphasis in Taoism on the way of nature is at the forefront of the kickback against monotheistic, monolithic ways of thinking. What is unexpected is that ecological concerns are providing a concrete context within which the theological protest becomes real. As climate change becomes more evident, as the science predicts, and as China becomes more conscious of the threats that it poses to the happiness and harmony of its people, it will be fascinating to watch how Taoism comes into its own.

Will God come at the end of time?

7

Buried in the DNA of some of the twenty-first century's most successful companies, organizations such as Google, lies an idea of God. It is called the Singularity. The Singularity refers to a moment in time, envisaged in the near future, in which a vast computer with cosmic intelligence will spring into being. This radically new kind of being will have the omnipotence and omniscience traditionally associated with God.

Marvin Minsky is one of the leading thinkers in the field of artificial intelligence (AI), whom Isaac Asimov described as one of the two people who were smarter than him, the other being Carl Sagan. He tells a story that describes this day, perhaps three decades into the twenty-first century, when computers will be able to replicate themselves with improvements and upgrades. The next generation of silicon machines will then do the same, starting a virtuous spiral of improving AI. Each repetition will come more quickly than the last. The process will accelerate exponentially. The net result is that suddenly, so far as humble humanity is concerned, robots with minds infinitely superior to our own will appear on earth. In that singular moment, they will rule us.

The story appears in various guises. Since the birth of the internet, it has been envisaged as some day coming alive. Some information technology futurists hope that the supreme AI will look kindly upon its ailing human parent and offer its vast databanks as a new home for the biological consciousness that otherwise dies with its host body, like a god bestowing resurrection and immortality. Ray Kurzweil, the inventor of optical character recognition technology, calculates the Singularity date as 2045. (He regularly updates the prediction, which can be tracked on the internet.) 'The coming Singularity is a popular belief in the society of technologists', writes Jaron Lanier, who coined the phrase 'virtual reality'. He is a Singularity sceptic, and adds in his book *You Are Not A Gadget*: 'Singularity books are as common in a computer science department as Rapture images are in an evangelical bookstore.'

A number of critics challenge the anticipation of this apocalyptic tipping point. Paul Allen, the co-founder of Microsoft, has explained that the Singularity isn't near because the so-called law of accelerating returns, by which computer power achieves the predicted runaway point, is not a law at all. It is, rather, a prediction based upon the past, and the past is not a good indicator of the future.

Alternatively, it is possible to question the AI assumption that human intelligence has been, or soon will be, replicated by computers, so that all that stands between here and the Singularity is faster soft- and hardware. Experts in human cognition routinely conclude the opposite: if the history of AI to date has shown us anything, it is that human cognition is still largely a mystery. Take just one thing that we have and computers don't, and it seems won't, according to the philosopher Hubert Dreyfus: imagination. Computers don't imagine the world and live in it, as we do. Instead, they proceed by trying to gather all the facts that there are in the world, and all the relationships between those facts, and then run algorithms that plot a course through that infinite tangle. It is a strategy that doesn't work. Imagination beats it every time, except in the case of very limited, artificial 'worlds'. Hence, computers are very good at chess and very bad at answering the most basic, everyday questions. Try typing, 'Is it sunny?' into Google. The computer will return nonsense. All we have to do is look outside.

Further, even in the world of chess, the fascinating thing is that human chess masters don't play the game in the way computers do. In fact, computers don't play the game at all. It is not a game for them, unless you call the equivalent of counting all the grains of sand in the Sahara a game, for such is the unimaginable drudgery that the poor computer has to embark upon before it says 'knight to c6'. Except that the computer has no imagination, so it experiences no drudgery; it experiences nothing.

A different test is proposed by John Gray. In *The Immortalisation Commission: The Strange Quest to Cheat Death*, he charts several instances in which science has been deployed to achieve traditional religious ends, like immortality. It is as if faith in the old gods has waned but human beings, out of need or habit, seek new sources of optimism in beings superior to themselves. Science provides rich soil for such fantasies, given its obvious record of success. But, Gray argues, what scientific optimism ignores is reality. Cast your mind back across history, he suggests, and even a schoolboy will know that nothing lasts forever. Human civilizations rise and fall within decades. Then, there are the longer periods of geological time during which the entire surface of the earth is remade. Mountains do not survive these huge forces; why should delicate computers? The old religions are right about one thing: if immortality is to be had, it will be found outside of time, which is why religions tend to hold out the hope not of immortality but of eternity.

The Singularity proposition does not stand up to much scrutiny, practical or theological. But its proponents have a trump card: the future. It is unknown. It is a blank slate onto which all manner of wishes can be projected and fulfilled. Computer science writes promissory notes that guarantee vast intelligence will be delivered at some moment down the line. And because they are located in the future, such promissory notes cannot be refuted. It is striking that even sceptics, such as Lanier, cannot quite write off the possible prospect. 'There might be some truth to the ideas associated with the Singularity at the very largest scale of reality', he adds, hedging his bets. 'It might be true that on some vast cosmic basis, higher and higher forms of consciousness inevitably arise, until the whole universe becomes a brain, or something along those lines.'

A related scenario has been championed by the writer Robert Wright, most recently in his book *The Evolution of God*. He has argued that the most significant discovery of the twentieth century was not biological, Watson and Crick's discovery of DNA, but economic. It is called game theory and is associated with the mathematician John von Neumann. It opens up another aspect of the Singularity-type questing for God characteristic of the scientistic faith of the twenty-first century.

Game theory is a complex discipline, but, in essence, the notion is that when two or more players engage in some kind of encounter that involves an exchange of information, they can choose a variety of strategies that have predictable outcomes. Some strategies will result in a win–lose situation: one person wins and the other loses, the winner winning at the loser's expense. However, other strategies result in a win–win situation: both individuals can walk away from the game having gained.

Wright proposes that game theory is embedded in the processes of evolution. Adaptive advantages and reproductive success – the mechanisms that allow organisms to survive and that lend nature the appearance of being designed – represent win–win strategies. They can be grouped together and called cases of win–win cooperation, examples of which abound in nature. You might point to anything from the mitochondria symbiosis in eukaryotic cells to the relationship between insects and plants, whereby insects feed on pollen and plants are pollinated by the feeding of the insects.

Win–win has the advantage over win–lose in that it sustains rather than destroys life. Further, win–win inclines towards increasing complexity in nature, as cooperation tends to build the intricacy of nature's patterns of mutuality and cooperation. The net result is that, over time, life can be said to progress. At first, this occurs at a biological level, witnessed in the movement of life from physiologically simple organisms to more complicated ones. There is also a corresponding emergence of mental phenomena that begin with simple interactions and evolve into awareness, then consciousness, then self-consciousness. As a result of this last really quite astonishingly complex capacity, the effects of win–win can be felt in the forms of culture and history too. Thus, and not without substantial setbacks and wrong turnings, human beings developed a moral sense, manifest in cooperation between civilizations, not just war. All manner of other moral gains finally triumph too. From the modern period, there would be anything from the abolition of slaves to the enfranchisement of women.

But why stop there? Wright proposes that the development of the monotheistic traditions is symptomatic of the higher reaches of the win–win result of moral improvement. He highlights the adoption of the Stoic notion of the logos, the benign, divine principle that runs through all things and draws them inexorably towards its final, good purposes. As we have seen, the Stoic idea was adopted by the Jewish philosopher, Philo, to expand his notion of God. It also appealed to the first Christian theologians. It appeals to Wright, too, who translates it in the economic language of game theory as 'the divine algorithm'.

Where Wright differs theologically is that, for him, the notion of God is almost certainly a construct of the human imagination. God does not reveal Godself in the great traditions of faith. Rather, God emerges as win–win outcomes become highly sophisticated, and is then adopted as a necessary fiction that further propels moral development.

As with the Singularity, a number of questions arise when game theory is connected to moral progress. It is possible to question the appeal to progress. Wasn't the twentieth century one of the bloodiest on record, what with the murderous regimes of Stalin, Mao and Hitler to name only the top three? Didn't the peace of the Cold War that followed the Second World War rest on the threat of global mutual annihilation should a nuclear holocaust erupt with full fury? Are not these signs not of progress but of extravagant regress? It is striking that Wright does not mention such dark characters in his book.

Conversely, you could question the assumption that ancient religions are somehow more primitive. Did not Picasso walk into the caves of Lascaux, observe the Paleolithic images of horses and bison, of bears and stags, and retort, 'We have discovered nothing'? Or, as we have seen in relation to the plural theology of Taoism, it is far from clear that monotheism automatically delivers unadulterated ethical advance.

But the myth of moral progress, like the open promises of the future, is seductive. It is almost irresistible in an age of science because it resonates so strongly with the onward march of scientific knowledge. Wright's thesis has been taken on by the psychologist Martin Seligman, the former president of the American Psychological Association and 'inventor' of positive psychology, also known as the science of happiness. Seligman makes the eschatological momentum of a win–win world explicit.

Seligman is perhaps typical of many western intellectuals in that he is disenchanted with religion but boundless in his hope for humankind. In his book *Authentic Happiness* he writes:

> *I've never been able to choke down the idea of a supernatural God who stands outside of time, a God who designs and creates the universe. As much as I wanted to, I [have] never been able to believe there was any meaning in life beyond the meaning we choose to adopt for ourselves. But now I'm beginning to think I was wrong, or partly wrong.*

He raises the possibility that the win–win genius of evolution presents a nascent theology that sceptics might accept because it can be backed by evidence. Reading Wright, he confesses to feeling

> *for the very first time the intimations of something vastly larger than I am or that human beings are. I have intimations of a God that those of us who are long on evidence and short on revelation (and long on hope, but short on faith) can believe in.*

This God would come at the end of time, at the end of the long evolutionary selection process. With increasing biological and cultural complexity comes ever-growing power and knowledge. And because of the benign effects of win–win, this evolution will also bring greater goodness, perhaps reaching a point when all is good. The God of traditional monotheism is realized in time. Seligman describes it this way:

> *in the very longest run, where is the principle of win–win headed? Toward a God who is not supernatural, a God who ultimately acquires omnipotence,*

omniscience, and goodness through the natural progress of win–win. Perhaps, just perhaps, God comes at the end.

It is a possibility that generates some meaning for Seligman, as it allows him to envisage his own work on happiness within the much larger 'project' of the cosmos.

There is one element that Seligman wishes to ditch, namely the concept of God as creator. This generates insurmountable theological hurdles for him, not only because a creator divinity is closely associated in his mind with a designer divinity, and evolution resists innate design, but more importantly because a creator must also be responsible for evil.

▲ The universe will come to an end, according to current cosmology, in either a 'big crunch' or an endless expansion to virtual nothingness.

He toys with process theology as a way around the problem of evil. 'The God of process theology gives up omnipotence and omniscience to allow human beings to enjoy free will', he writes. 'To circumvent "who created the Creator", process theology gives up creation itself by claiming that the process of becoming more complex just goes on forever; there was no beginning and will be no end.' On the other hand, process theology does not entirely satisfy him because its vision of divinity is attenuated. He continues: 'This leaves us with the idea of a God who had nothing whatever to do with creation, but who is omnipotent, omniscient, and righteous'.

Process theology

Process theology has a radically dynamic view of God. God is envisaged as being the deepest manifestation of the process of change that runs through all things.

It is a direct rejection of traditional Christian theology, which, drawing on the metaphysics of the ancient Greeks, viewed changelessness as more fundamental than changeability. It was reasoned that God must be changeless because God is perfect: if God changes then God could only change for the better, which implies that God would have been less than perfect before, which the divine perfection disallows.

Process theologians, drawing on the twentieth-century philosophy of A N Whitehead alongside others, argue that change is real. Changelessness is not. Much as the natural world is seen to evolve, through processes that include suffering and experiment, so God is in process too. God is seeking to bring creation to its fulfilment, though not in a deterministic way: the details of that fulfilment are not predicted ahead of time, much as the complexity of the natural world emerges in time.

Whitehead refers to God as the 'Principle of Concretion', or that which selects and makes the possible actual or concrete. In the chapter on God in his book *Science and the Modern World*, he notes that 'every actual occasion is a limitation imposed on possibility, and that by virtue of this limitation the particular value of that shaped togetherness of things emerges'. According to this logic, there is no such thing as a beautiful sunset in the abstract, but only the beautiful sunset that fell between such and such a time, in such and such a place. It came and went. It was a process. Similarly, with all things that are valued because they are good, beautiful or true, they are so because they are particular.

The course of creation is, therefore, the process of what is made real, reality being that which exists necessarily within limits. 'Restriction is the price paid for value', Whitehead explains, and so God can be called 'the ultimate limitation': so far as human beings are concerned, God is experienced in the process, in the concrete, in the limited.

This accounts for the diversity of religious experiences. 'In respect to the interpretation of these experiences, mankind has differed profoundly', he explains. 'He has been named respectively, Jehovah, Allah, Brahma, Father in Heaven, Order of Heaven, First Cause, Supreme Being, Chance. Each name corresponds to a system of thought derived from the experiences of those who have used it.'

Once again, the validity of this 'hope in God' rests on the validity of the science that underpins it, this time not computer science but economics. If you buy the belief in moral progress, and game theory, then it may be persuasive. Similarly, it is open to the critique that has been offered of process theology – a critique that Seligman is clearly aware of; that it leaves God stripped of at least some of the powers usually associated with divinity. Is it right to worship a God who is not perfect, a Judeo-Christian or Islamic believer might ask. Is that not called idolatry? Alternatively, belief in a God who has nothing to do with creation, day by day, is usually referred to as deism. It describes a divinity whose role is setting natural laws and cosmic limits before withdrawing to allow creation to unfold. This is not the theist God who actively sustains creation moment by moment.

It is interesting that Seligman seems happy to countenance a divinity with no creative powers, though requires one that represents the totality of knowledge, power and goodness. That might be called a 'God of the scientists' as it captures science's highest aspirations, much like the 'God of the philosophers', which represents all that philosophy most admires.

A final critique could play the future card against the future, as it were, by speculating that if this omniscience, omnipotent force emerges at the end of time, why wouldn't this extraordinary power transcend the normal passage of time? This deity would not need to be held by the limits of its genesis. Once it appeared, wouldn't it immediately fill the whole of space and time, retrogressively, perhaps along the lines of backwards causation in quantum physics? Which is to ask whether that God is not already with us.

That is the power of the promissory notes written with guarantees set in the distant future. That is its unsatisfactory nature as the basis for theology. It's fun, but when almost anything can be envisaged as possible, reality comes to feel unreal.

The God of well-being

Part of the reason that the God of moral progress appeals to modern people such as Martin Seligman and Robert Wright may be that links between human well-being and spiritual advance have become a central theme in consumer society. The speculations of Seligman and Wright are possibly more refined. But they chime with ideas from the New Age, which is perhaps why their books become popular bestsellers.

Consider the use of the word 'spiritual' in *The Body Care Manual*, published by the high-street chain The Body Shop. It tells us that aromatherapy has been used to promote 'physical, emotional, and spiritual health' for at least 6000 years. Similarly, massage can ease physical, mental and spiritual ailments. The manual advocates retreats and walks as a way of reconnecting with your spiritual self.

This may well be true. What is theologically interesting, though, is the way the advocacy of such spiritual health involves a rejection of western traditions in favour of those from the east, which are promoted as 'alternative'. In this sense, this theology of well-being mirrors Seligman's rejection of the traditional notions of God. The old is critiqued or passed over in favour of something new.

Another similarity is that established science is deployed to lend credence to theological speculation. In the case of Wright and Seligman, evolution is appealed to. In the broader arena of the New Age, all manner of scientific discourses may be drawn on. So-called 'quantum healing', say, borrows from quantum physics to argue that, at base, nature is a constant flux of energy. Practitioners of quantum healing can manipulate energy packages within the human body, and thereby bring benefit. That eastern medicine deploys dynamic concepts of somatic energy builds a sense that there must be something in it.

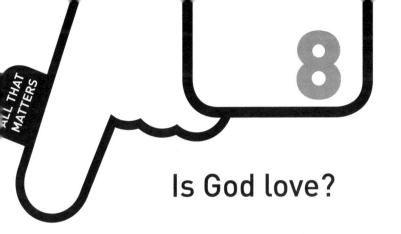

8

Is God love?

Love, according to Sigmund Freud, will misfire. It is an instinctual force that propels us towards other people and things, and that means it inevitably comes into conflict with its opposites, hate and fear. Thus, it is readily inhibited and perverted. Iris Murdoch caught some of the tension when she observed that, 'Love is the painful realisation that something other than myself exists.'

And yet, there is also a strong sense in Freud that love is deeper than hate or fear. Without love, there could be no hate or fear, for they are premised on the desire to love: they are misfirings of love. It is as if love is not an instinct, but life itself. And that is basic. 'Life in its innermost nature goes we know not where', reflects the psychoanalyst Neville Symington.

Theologians would be inclined to agree with this primordial intuition. It reaches way back. There was a powerful strand in ancient Greek theology which held that Eros was the first god. It is expressed by Hesiod, a poet of the eighth and seventh centuries BCE, in his *Theogony*, concerning the origins of the gods and the cosmos. Love plays a key role for him because procreation is the source of new life, which is to say that love is the source of life. 'Love is a great god', Phaedrus says in Plato's *Symposium*, reflecting on this tradition, 'Wonderful in many ways to gods and men, and most marvellous of all is the way he came into being. We honour him as one of the most ancient gods, and the proof of his great age is this; the parents of Love have no place in poetry or legend.'

The fundamental, divine nature of love is picked up by the presocratic philosophers, Parmenides and Empedocles.

Parmenides is remembered as writing, 'The very first god designed was Love'. Empedocles conceives of the cosmos as in the grip of an epic cycle, powered by a continuous struggle between love and strife. Love is that constructive force which pervades all things. Strife would bring about the opposite and is a sinister, destructive tendency. Love must be amongst the first of the gods, Empedocles reasons, because earth is joined to Heaven in a union cemented by love.

It is a moving myth, in several senses. It helps express, in a mix of mythology and proto-science, an inescapable feature of everyday life. We live in a state in which love and strife compete. No individual, or society, is in a state of harmony, but rather finds itself to be shot through with difference – though that difference makes us what we are. Life is a constant attempt to 'gather up the fragments', to embrace it all in love. Love has prevailed in the past and will prevail again, Empedocles insists, but for now we must contend with the conflicts of life, whilst nurturing the hope of union that love brings.

Another feature to note is how love operates within nature. Eros can bring about good effects, Empedocles stresses, only by remaining within the whirl of life, by engaging with strife. This is a psychological truth: love must contend with hate and fear, its misfirings. It is also an empirical claim: the ways of love, and hence the ways of the gods, can be discerned by observing the ways of the world and the minds of men and women.

This was done by Thales, sometimes called the father of western philosophy. Only one of his complete utterances

▲ Teresa of Avila in her erotic ecstasy, as depicted by Bernini, is shown being pierced by the love of God in the spear thrust by the angel.

comes down to us, though it is a good one: 'Everything is full of gods.' It can be interpreted in several ways, but a good guess as to what he meant arrives in relation to his interest in magnets. The power of magnets drew him, Aristotle records, because magnets have attractive, unifying capacities. They move one another by some innate force or instinct, such as love. Thales saw the world as full of gods, then, because everything in the world is seen to move. Nothing stands still. This mysterious life tendency is a sign of divine influence, that the world has an animating soul. There is a sense in which everything is alive. That is what the god Love achieves too.

The Christian theologian, L William Countryman, translates the old mythology into a modern, monotheistic idiom. In his book *Love Human and Divine* he writes:

> *[Love] brings us into communion not only with God and with one another, but with every element in creation, from rocks to seraphim. Whether your connection with rocks takes the forms of a collector's enthusiasm, a scientific delight in geology, an experience of mysticism in the natural world, or a sculptor's intimacy with marble is secondary. Whether your relatedness with another human takes the form of a lifelong nonsexual friendship or a lifelong sexual partnership, shared membership on a team or mutual esteem in the workplace, a sibling relationship or the bond of teacher and student, they all proceed from the same erotic power of relating.*

That is life, it is love, and, for believers, it is God.

Divine love in Indian philosophy

The Hindu god of love is Kama, often depicted as a young man whose flowery arrows provoke love in those they pierce. His great cosmic achievement was making Shiva, the god of destruction and transformation, fall in love with Parvati, an altogether more gentle and temperate consort.

Kama is also viewed as a personification of one of the great ends of life, a love of the sensual and aesthetic, a delight in the physical and the spiritual. Just how to achieve this end, without offending the teachings of the dharma, is explored in the *Kama Sutra*, the classic textbook of the arts of loving in Indian philosophy.

Plato's ideas about love are crucial in the monotheist religions of Islam, Judaism and Christianity. He challenges much of what he received from his own tradition.

In the *Symposium*, he has Diotima, a priestess who instructs Socrates in the 'arts of loving', argue that love cannot be a god. This is because love is a form of desire, and you only desire what you lack, be it that which is good, that which is beautiful or that which is true. Gods do not lack anything, so love must be a go-between, a benign demon. Diotima continues, explaining how demons work:

> *They are messengers who shuttle back and forth between [gods and mortals], conveying prayer and sacrifice from men to gods, while to men they bring commands from the gods and gifts in return for sacrifices. Being in the middle of the two, they round out the whole and bind fast the all to all . . . Gods do not mix with men; they mingle and converse with us through spirits instead, whether we are awake or asleep. He who is wise in any of these ways is a man of the spirit, but he who is wise in any other way, in a profession or any manual work, is merely a mechanic. These spirits are many and various, then, and one of them is Love.*

It is a fascinating move. The gods are conceived of as transcendent and different from men and women, mediating between the two realms, enabled by love. Hence, too, in monotheistic theologies it is common to find that God is hidden from rational conception, though known by more primitive intuitions like love.

The tradition is particularly well developed in eastern Orthodox theology, where God's ousia, or being – God as God is – is distinct from the energies of God, which is the love of God we humans might experience. We can know the latter, but not the former, because the ousia 'finds no existence or subsistence in another or any other thing', as Vladimir Lossky puts it in 'The Mystical Theology of the Eastern Church'. It is out of human reach because, echoing Spinoza's insight that God is 'a substance consisting of infinite attributes, each of which expresses eternal and infinite essence', God is God's own cause.

God's energies though, supremely so in the case of love, are felt and known by human beings. Plato makes it the heart of his philosophy. In several dialogues, he implies that if you stir up the capacity to love inside you, and apply reason to direct your love in the right way, then you might achieve an understanding of what is good, beautiful and true. Anthony Price, in his book *Love and Friendship in Plato and Aristotle*, describes the role of love in this way: 'Love may be the best helper not because it provides reasons, but because, in a promising soul well prompted, it is receptive of, and responsive to, the opening of new vistas.'

Love and prayer in Islam

Islam teaches that the daily prayers offered to God must be performed in love, a yearning for Allah. The recitation begins with 'Allahu akbar' ('God is great'), with a hand on the chest that is then raised. Next the Muslim bows, with hands on knees, before reciting 'God is great' again, and then 'Praise be to God the sublime'. Complete prostrations follow, as a sign of submission to God, with short recitations and exaltations. They are embodied efforts to orientate the will and the desire of the faithful away from the self-centred concerns of the ego and towards the divine.

Directed correctly, love draws you out of yourself too. It nurtures a passion for that which is beautiful, which in Plato's view of the world is also that which is good and true. This process is known as the 'ascent of love'. It is no easy path to follow; it takes a long time. Diotima describes it as being full of toils, and it can also go horribly wrong. (Freud was a reader of 'the Divine Plato' too, as he referred to the ancient Greek.) However, there is always the possibility that a lover can be awakened to other kinds of beauty, as, say, inherent in the insights of science or the arts; and then they may become alert to the beauty of truth. Finally, at the pinnacle of the ascent, the 'goal of loving', that which is 'wonderfully beautiful in its nature', is seen. An 'eye of the soul' has been opened to Plato's conception of God.

Eastern Orthodoxy is in direct continuity with this tradition. It too understands divine knowledge as an erotic affair, 'the achievement and gift of an erotic relationship', as the theologian Christos Yannaras describes it in *On the Absence and Unknowability of God*. He stresses that knowing God is not primarily a matter of learning. It is one of passion, in the sense of that which is suffered.

The link between loving God and suffering arises because human beings are powerfully wedded to their own self-sufficiency. As Freud understood, it is vital in infancy that we love ourselves to the exclusion of everything else, in order that we might survive. He wittily referred to 'His Majesty the Baby'. But growing up is necessary too: the painful struggle to recognize others. That begins in parent–child relations and reaches a pitch in the passionate quest for God. This is the most fearful yearning, Yannaras stresses, a form of ecstasy, literally meaning a stepping out of yourself. That is hard, though only with such difficult self-transcendence comes divine relationship.

▲ Michelangelo's depiction of God giving life to Adam, from the Sistine Chapel, which the art historian Vasari described as 'a figure whose beauty, pose and contours are such that it seems to have been fashioned that very moment by the first and supreme creator'.

There is a second reason that love, for human beings, is painful. We are flawed, fallen. Human love is prone to collapse, to the hatreds and inhibitions so widely charted by Freud and his successors. But although Freud himself denied it, he being a committed atheist, the Christian hope is that a perfected love is possible in the yearning for God, because God loves us first. There is a top-down dynamic that matches the bottom-up of human love.

This is another radical development from Plato. In Plato, the love of the good, beautiful and true is an upward motion, though at the pinnacle of the ascent it is an impersonal divine that is glimpsed. As union is experienced, the erotic dimension to the experience ceases because what has been desired is, finally, gained. Love ceases. Christianity teaches otherwise because it makes the further step of declaring not just that love is a demon or god, but that the God of monotheism is love. Yannaras again:

> The unique identity of Christian revelation . . . is this experience of God as the 'mad lover' of the whole creation and of each human person. God, not as the abstract idea of the highest Good, not as the concept of the 'first cause' of existent beings, nor as the intimidating image of implacable justice, but God as Person in a 'transport of erotic goodness' is the 'good news', the gospel of the Church, the message of its experience.

Human understanding of the first god, Love, has shifted subtly over time. The earliest intimations that love was at the base of life, because love fires creation, joined hands with the sense that love is in a cosmic battle. It struggles with that which causes division and strife, and longs to draw all things into union. Plato, arguably the greatest lover of love – in the strict sense of yearning to know and understand love – develops a vision of love as a transcendent force, carrying the human lover to higher reaches of experience that are at once intimately woven into the ways of the world. The Christian view of things adds another dimension, that of the personal. God is not just discovered in passionate love but is discovered to be love. God is love. 'Unknowable and unapproachable in his essence, God . . . is revealed as a personal energy of erotic longing for each of his creatures', Yannaras concludes.

We should leave the last word in this lovely vision to Yannaras's own main theological inspiration, the early church mystic Denys the Aeropagite. Here is his 'definition' of God:

> The very cause of the universe in the beautiful, good superabundance of his benign eros for all is carried outside of himself . . . beguiled, as it were, by goodness, by love, and by eros and is enticed away from his transcendence of all things and beyond all things and comes to abide within all things, and he does so by virtue of his supernatural and ecstatic capacity to remain, nevertheless, within himself.

Appendix: A note on the proofs

The so-called proofs for the existence of God are widely thought to fail.

Philosophers point out that there is no need for an 'unmoved mover', to use Aristotle's phrase. Thomas Aquinas considers this as the first of the five 'ways' that people tend to talk about God, but it seems redundant now because modern physics teaches us that motion is the default state of matter, not stasis.

Alternatively, the so-called ontological argument comes to look like a conjuring trick with words. Anselm said that God must be that than which nothing greater can be conceived, and wondered whether this shows God exists because, if God didn't exist, the divine greatness would be compromised. But it is no more the case that God needs to exist because God's imagined greatness demands it, than it is the case that a perfect island needs to exist because it is described as perfect. Both might be fantasy.

As for the argument from design – the notion that the apparent purpose, fit and beauty of the natural world requires a designer – that can be dismissed in a single word: evolution. Darwinian processes of natural selection produce the illusion of design by a combination of random change and environmental filtering, at least when it comes to the living world.

So far, so familiar for students of the philosophy of religion. What is not widely observed, though, is that the failure of the 'proofs' is only what theists should expect. They might even be glad of it. There are a number of reasons why proofs that worked would actually lessen, not increase, the appeal of religious belief.

For one thing, a deity that could be proven to exist would, by implication, be a deity that was comprehensible to the human mind. To be able successfully to reason the existence of a god would necessitate being able to understand the reasons for the existence of that god.

Religious traditions have a word for such theological confidence. It is idolatry. The only gods that human beings can fully grasp are gods that human beings have made in their own image. Hence, idolatry is the worst sin in the Bible, second only to usury. Believers should expect purported proofs ultimately to fail – for all that many interesting thoughts might be generated by the effort – because the proofs are, inevitably, human proofs.

Put it this way. There is a reason that God is described as 'immortal', because whatever God might be – and who knows? – God is certainly not mortal. Similarly, God is said to be 'invisible': whatever God might be, God is not visible. This kind of God-talk says nothing about God's actual attributes, and so nothing that might contribute to a proof. Rather it focuses on how God seems from the perspective of the finite and visible mortals who seek to know God. How could it be otherwise?

A similar point can be expressed in more existential terms. If God were completely and transparently obvious to the human mind, then would not the human experience of God be terrifying and tyrannical? Direct experience of, say, divine omnipotence – should it turn out that God were all-powerful, whatever that might mean – would obliterate human freedom. To feel the full force of divine omniscience – again, supposing for the sake of argument there is such a theological quality – would belittle human striving. It would be like living with an overbearing parent, who would limit your chances at becoming fully human simply by their presence, for all that they loved you.

This must be the reason that the Bible talks about the impossibility of being able to see God and live, or that it is the fear of the Lord, not the comprehension of the Lord, that is the beginning of wisdom.

A different reason why it is important that the proofs fail is that it makes clear that the human quest for the divine is not a purely rational pursuit. If that were the case, if God could be discovered by logic, then the spiritual quest would be a demoralising, dispiriting affair. What role then for the emotions, for the arts, for the darkness, for the revelatory, for the continual discovery? If reason could tell all, then reason would rule all, and that would surely leave us less than human.

In truth, whether or not you believe in God is primarily a matter of the heart, not the head – the heart understood metaphorically as the place where we humans attempt to integrate the panoply of our thought, intuition, experience, evidence. Reason will have a star role in the process of discernment; but reason of itself needs something else to go on. Proofs cannot pull themselves up by their own bootstraps.

What then do the 'proofs' actually achieve? Aquinas summed it up well. All that we have proven, he says, is that the fundamental nature of divinity is mystery. Religious belief, then, is the attempt to cultivate a relationship with that mystery. That is the gift of the proofs' failure.

50 key theological thinkers and spiritual practitioners

1 **Abraham (c. 2000–1650 BCE)** Wanderer from the town of Ur, who settled in Canaan and became the father of the three monotheistic faiths, Judaism, Christianity and Islam.

2 **Abu Bakr (c. 570–634 CE)** Father of the Prophet's beloved wife, Aishah, and successor to Muhammad honoured by Sunni Muslims.

3 **Ali (d. 661 CE)** Cousin and son-in-law of Muhammad who is honoured by Shi'ite Muslims as the rightful successor to the Prophet.

4 **Aristotle (384–322 BCE)** Pupil of Plato, whose wide-ranging philosophical and empirical interests reshaped western theology during the medieval period.

5 Augustine of Hippo (354–430 CE) Towering Christian theologian whose spiritual autobiography, *The Confessions*, is a classic of world literature.

6 Averroës (1126–98 CE) Muslim philosopher whose commentaries on Aristotle became crucial in Christian Europe as Aristotle's writings came to the west.

7 Avicenna (980–1037 CE) Arab polymath who is regarded as the most important figure in Islam's golden age, synthesizing Islam with Aristotelian and Platonic philosophies.

8 Bahaullah (1817–92 CE) Persian organizer of the Baha'i faith, previously a Shi'ite movement, which teaches that God is one and that humankind is destined for unity.

9 Bodhidharma (6th century CE) Probable founder of the Zen school of Buddhism, the 'direct transmission of awakened consciousness, outside tradition or scripture'.

10 Buddhaghosa (5th century CE) Author of *Visuddhimagga*, 'The Path of Purification', which provides a synthesis of many teachings of Buddhism found in the Pali Canon.

11 Chu His (1130–1200 CE) Figure in neo-Confucianism, which embraces the notion of T'ai Chi, the principle of heaven and earth, which in turn gives rise to Yang (movement) and Yin (emptiness).

12 Chuang Tzu (369-286 BCE) The originator of what is called philosophical Taoism, which includes the principle of wu wei, or 'non-action' in life and ethics.

13 Confucius (5th–6th century BCE) Chinese minister who spent much of his life wandering and became better known as a teacher who advocated traditional values.

14 David Hume (1711–76) Scottish philosopher of the Enlightenment, now remembered in religious discussions for his critique of design in creation and miracles.

15 Dogen (1200–1253) Key figure in the Soto Zen tradition, which emphasizes the practice of sitting meditation, or zazen, to gain enlightenment.

16 Eisai (1141–1215) Founder of the Rinzai form of Zen, which aims to shock adherents into a deeper appreciation of the truth of reality.

17 Epicurus (c. 341–270 BCE) Founder of Epicurean philosophy, who taught followers not to fear gods, death or pain, and to love simple goods such as water and friendship.

18 Francis Bacon (1561–1626) Lord Chancellor of England whose philosophy of learning underpins modern science and taught divine sanction for human dominion in nature.

19 Friedrich Nietzsche (1844–1900) German philosopher who sought to overturn conventional Christian morality and announced the 'death of God'.

20 Ghazali (1058–1111) Muslim philosopher who became a Sufi mystic, following a breakdown, and sought to integrate Islamic philosophy and law.

21 Hillel (1st century BCE to 1st century CE) Respected Jewish teacher who became very influential in Rabbinic Judaism, after the end of temple-based Judaism.

22 Honen (1133–1212) Figure associated with Pure Land Buddhism, which holds that Amida Buddha saves all things and this recognition, not personal effort, wins enlightenment.

23 Hsun Tzu (4th to 3rd centuries BCE) Confucian thinker who argued for an impersonal conception of heaven that can be identified with nature and reason.

24 Jesus of Nazareth (c. 6/5 BCE to c. 30 CE) Reformist Jew whose example and teachings, death and resurrection inspired his followers, subsequently called Christians, to believe he is God incarnate.

25 Kapila (1st century BCE to 2nd century CE) Traditional founder of the Sankhya school in Hinduism and probably the oldest, focusing on suffering and liberation.

26 Karl Marz (1818–83) Philosopher of communism, who argued that religion was the opiate of the people, and so would disappear as material conditions improved.

27 Lao Tzu (6th century BCE or older) Meaning 'Old Master', the traditional author of the *Tao Te Ching* and founder of Taoism, which teaches how to live in the way.

28 Mahavira (6th or 5th century BCE) Ascetic teacher who inspired Jainism, the Indian religion that gives central place to the theory and practice of non-violence.

29 Maimonides (1135–1204) Sephardic Jewish philosopher, with wide influence outside Judaism, whose *Guide to the Perplexed* synthesizes Judaism and Aristotelianism.

30 Martin Luther (1483–1546) Priest whose indignation at the excesses of the Roman Catholic indulgences system led to attacks on the Pope and inspired the Reformation.

31 Mencius (390–305 BCE) Confucian thinker who developed the notion of jen, or humaneness, into a system of moral self-cultivation.

32 Moses (15th to 13th centuries BCE) Traditional author of the first five books of the Hebrew Bible and leader of the ancient Israelites out of Egypt into the Promised Land.

33 Muhammad (c. 570–632 CE) Arab prophet honoured by Muslims, and recipient of the final revelation of God received over a period of 23 years, gathered in the Qur'an.

34 Nagarjuna (2nd century CE) Founder of the Madhyamaka school of Buddhism, one of the principal traditions within Mahayana, which means 'middle way' and emphasizes emptiness.

35 Nanak (1439–1539) First of the 10 gurus who founded the Sikh faith, following a mystical experience, and taught the unity of the human spirit and the love of God.

36 Padmasambhava (8th century CE) Quasi-legendary Tantric teacher who founded Tibetan Buddhism in the Nyingmapa school that embraces siddhi or 'magical powers'.

37 Patanjali (2nd century BCE to 4th century CE) Author of the 'Yoga Sutra', the oldest Yoga text, which contain sets of spiritual disciplines promising liberation.

38 Paul (d. c. 64/68 CE) Jewish rabbi, also known as Saul of Tarsus, who had a visionary experience of the risen Jesus, subsequently taking Christianity to non-Jewish peoples.

39 Plato (c. 428–347 CE) Pupil of Socrates and his greatest interpreter; his teachings in the Greek Academy and dialogues nurtured a love of the good, beautiful and true.

40 Rabiah (713–801 CE) Muslim mystic, honoured amongst Sufis. She taught in pithy aphorisms and practised unification with God through love.

41 Ramanuja (1017–1137 CE) Teacher of the Visistadvaita Indian tradition who held that religious devotion leads to a relationship with a personal God.

42 Saicho (767–822 CE) Promoter of Tendai Buddhism in Japan, which argues that all religious teachings lead to enlightenment because all that is necessary is a commitment to one path or another.

43 Sankara (c. 788–820 CE) Author of the *Brahmasutrabhasya*, one of the most important works of Indian philosophy, claiming that the world as we perceive it is illusion.

44 Siddhartha Gautama (563–483 BCE) Later to be called the Buddha, or fully awakened one, he was an Indian aristocrat who, troubled by suffering, found a means to overcome it.

45 Socrates (740–399 BCE) Citizen of Athens who had a vocation from the god Apollo to reveal how human beings might live well, based upon understanding the depths of their ignorance.

46 Tenzin Gyatso (b. 1935) The fourteenth Dalai Lama, who has championed the cause of Tibetans in exile and sparked interest in Tibetan Buddhism around the world.

47 Thomas Aquinas (1225–74) Dominican monk and subtle Christian philosophical theologian who reconciled Aristotle's thought with the western tradition.

48 Udayana (10th century CE) Philosopher of the Nyaya-Vaisesika school in Hinduism, who argued that God exists because the existence of the cosmos is an effect that cannot be its own cause.

49 Zeno of Citium (334–262 BCE) Founder of the Stoic school of philosophy, which teaches adherents to 'go with the flow' or be aligned with a benign, cosmic logos.

50 Zoroaster (c. 1000 BCE) Persian prophet who taught that Ahura Mazda, the one good God, is opposed by evil divinities, and is influential in the development of monotheism.

20 recommended books

. . . in addition to those referenced throughout this book:

51 *A History of God* by Karen Armstrong (Vintage, 1999) is a highly readable, well-informed large volume of ideas about God across the ages.

52 *Absence of Mind* by Marilynne Robinson (Yale University Press, 2010) is probably the best book to have emerged from the so-called 'God wars' of the twenty-first century.

53 *Chambers Dictionary of Beliefs and Religions* edited by Mark Vernon (Chambers, 2009) is a useful source book for the key figures, terms and disputes in world religions.

54 *Concepts of God: Images of the Divine in Five Religious Traditions* by Keith Ward (Oneworld, 1998) examines ideas from the Jewish tradition and Indian subcontinent in particular.

55 *Confessions* by Saint Augustine, translated by Garry Wills (Penguin, 2008), is the one book of original Christian theology and spirituality to be read above all others.

56 *Faith Seeking* by Denys Turner (SCM Press, 2002) is a collection of personal pieces from one of the most reflective and accessible contemporary philosophers of religion.

57 *God and the Processes of Reality* by David A Pailin (Routledge, 1989) presents a theology in accord with the increasingly influential ideas of process philosophy.

58 *No God But God: The Origins, Evolution and Future of Islam* by Reza Aslan (William Heinemann, 2005) is a passionate plea for a compassionate and authentic Islam.

59 *On Aquinas* by Herbert McCabe (Continuum, 2008) is a lucid introduction to this seminal Christian theologian.

60 *Philosophers and God: At the Frontiers of Faith and Reason* edited by John Cornwell and Michael McGhee (Continuum, 2009) contains fascinating essays by contemporary philosophers of religion.

61 *Religion in Human Evolution: From the Paleolithic to the Axial Age* by Robert Bellah (Belknap Harvard, 2011) has an excellent account of the latest evolutionary theories of the human quest for God.

62 *Science and Religion in Quest of Truth* by John Polkinghorne (SPCK, 2011) is an enlightening summary by a leading scientist of how theism is in accordance with modern science.

63 *Selling Spirituality: The Silent Takeover of Religion* by Jeremy Carrette and Richard King (Routledge, 2005) examines what happens when spiritual and divine matters enter the consumer marketplace.

64 *The Book of Chuang Tzu*, translated by Martin Palmer (Penguin Classics, 2006), includes a lively introduction to Taoism by this scholar of Chinese religions.

65 *The Faith to Doubt: Glimpses of Buddhist Uncertainty* by Stephen Batchelor (Parallax Press, 1990) is part spiritual tome and part travelogue, reflecting on an experience of Buddhist meditation.

66 *The Gay Science*, by Friedrich Nietzsche, translated by Walter Kaufmann (Vintage Books, 1974), is where he proclaims the 'death of God', and shows that he is still the best atheist to read.

67 *The Sovereignty of Good* by Iris Murdoch (Routledge Classics, 2001) presents a compelling vision of Platonism for the modern day.

68 *The Spiritual Dimension: Religion, Philosophy and Human Value* by John Cottingham (Cambridge University Press, 2005) provides a humane and spiritually sensitive introduction to the philosophy of religion.

69 *The Unknown God* by Anthony Kenny (Continuum, 2004) contains short essays in which one of the UK's leading philosophers explores his agnosticism.

70 *What is Ancient Philosophy?* by Pierre Hadot (Harvard University Press, 2004) is an important re-envisaging of Greek philosophy as it was; a spiritual quest and way of life.

10 places to visit

71 Jerusalem, Israel – the eternal city that is home to three world religions and whose streets positively buzz with humankind's passion for the divine.

72 The Basilica of San Clemente in Rome, which is remarkable for being both an ancient Christian church and a pre-Christian Mithraic temple.

73 Stonehenge, Wiltshire, England, the mystery of which can be keenly felt on a clear day when the sun is low in the sky.

74 Chartres Cathedral, France, and particularly the labyrinth near the west end, which graphically represents the tortuous journey of the soul back to its centre.

75 The cave Hira, on the mountain of Jabal al-Nour, near Mecca, is the place where the prophet Muhammad received his first revelations.

76 Angkor Wat, Siem Reap, Cambodia, which is a temple complex built in the twelfth century and matches any contemporary cathedral built in Europe.

77 The Temple of Heaven, Beijing, China. It is geographically linked to the Forbidden City, showing how the whole city was a kind of massive altar across which people approached the divine.

78 Columbia Hills, Washington, USA, the home of a striking collection of Native American rock art, known as petroglyphs.

79 Varanasi, Uttar Pradesh, India, considered to be the most holy place for Hindus, a religion that encourages pilgrimage with all the colour and excitement that brings.

80 Bodbgaya, Bihar, India, which is the site of the Bodhi tree, under which Gautama Buddha is said to have achieved enlightenment.

10 films to see

81 *The Ten Commandments* (1956), directed by Cecile B DeMille, is the landmark Hollywood religious blockbuster.

82 *The Gospel According to St Matthew* (1964), directed by Pier Paolo Pasolini, is one of the most moving filmic depictions of the life of Jesus of Nazareth.

83 *Life of Brian* (1979) is Monty Python's infamous take on Christianity, and a must-see for those interested in spiritual satire with an intelligent message.

84 *The Exorcist* (1999), directed by William Friedkin, which just goes to show that, even in a supposedly secular age, no-one beats the devil when it comes to horror.

85 *Siddartha* (1972) is Conrad Rooks's adaptation of the Herman Hesse novel of the same title, which explores the quest for life's answers in Indian traditions.

86 *The Mahabharata* (1989), directed by Peter Brooks, is a long but visually arresting telling of the Hindu text.

87 *Galileo* (1974) is Joseph Losey's adaptation of Bertolt Brecht's play that explores the conflict between the scientist of the heavens and the Catholic church.

88 *Fiddler on the Roof* (1971) is the musical story of a Jewish family's attempts to maintain their religious traditions as a persecutory, secular world rises around them.

89 *Gandhi* (1982), directed by Richard Attenborough and starring Ben Kingsley, is the definitive biopic of the prophet and leader's life.

90 *The Lord of the Rings* (2001–3), the trilogy directed by Peter Jackson, adapts J R R Tolkien's books to tell a psychological tale of descent into the shadow and darkness.

10 websites to browse

91 Internet Sacred Texts Archive (www.sacred-texts.com) offers a massive store of online religious texts to read and browse.

92 Beliefnet (www.beliefnet.com), one of the most visited spiritual websites on the planet.

93 FaithWorld (http://blogs.reuters.com/faithworld) offers top news and analysis from Reuters' best writers and commentators.

94 The Immanent Frame (http://blogs.ssrc.org/tif) is a site devoted to the latest academic research in the study of religions.

95 The Catholic Encyclopedia (www.newadvent.org/cathen/index.html), which does what it says on the cover.

96 The Virtual Religion Index (http://virtualreligion.net), from Rutgers University, is a guide to multifaith religious and theological resources on the internet.

97 The BBC's introduction to world religions (www.bbc.co.uk/religion/religions).

98 A Virtual Visit to the Sistine Chapel (www.vatican.va/various/cappelle/sistina_vr/index.html), which will reveal more artistic details than are possible to see during an actual visit.

99 Religion Dispatches (www.religiondispatches.org) is a provocative contemporary American news and comment site.

100 The Guardian's Cif Belief (www.guardian.co.uk/commentisfree/belief), for which the author regularly writes.

Note

Page 51

1 This chapter is, in part, a revised version of a series of articles on William James by Mark Vernon first published in the *Guardian*, used with permission.

ALL THAT MATTERS: GOD

Index

ALL THAT MATTERS: GOD